Contents

GW01471482

1 Introduction

The National Planning Policy Framework (NPPF) recognises the desirability and importance of securing the conservation of heritage assets and taking account of impacts upon them as part of the decision-taking process (MHCLG 2018).

Whilst piling has the potential to cause a high level of harm to archaeological remains, nonetheless, it forms one of the most commonly used methods of delivering sustainable development in challenging development conditions.

Foundation solutions that seek to preserve archaeological remains by avoiding and minimising harm, are an essential tool in ensuring that development can take place where archaeological remains are present, particularly where technical or economic factors might otherwise prevent development.

Planning background

The policies of the NPPF identify heritage assets, including archaeological remains, as an irreplaceable resource. Any harm to or loss of the significance of heritage assets requires clear and convincing justification; local planning authorities are required to consider how conflict between heritage assets' conservation and development might be avoided or minimised as part of their decision-taking process.

In all cases where development will lead to harm to or loss of heritage assets, the NPPF places the onus on the determining body to make a balanced judgement, taking account of the significance of the heritage asset affected, the scale of any harm or loss caused and any public benefits it would deliver. Through this process, it can be possible for development to take place in areas of high archaeological sensitivity by providing protection to the majority of the remains on site.

This guidance is intended to support and enable sustainable development to proceed, by ensuring that harm is avoided or minimised wherever possible and that where harm or loss can be justified, that the impact on archaeological deposits and artefacts is appropriately managed. Specifically, this document illustrates how piled foundations can play an important part in delivering the objectives set out in the policies of the NPPF, subject to an informed and cooperative design process.

This document follows and expands upon the approach set out within the Managing Significance in Decision-Taking in the Historic Environment: Historic Environment Good Practice Advice in Planning Note GPA2 (Historic England 2015). It should also be read in conjunction with Preserving Archaeological Remains, Decision-taking for Sites under Development (Historic England, 2016) which provides the overarching framework for decision taking on these types of sites. Both documents emphasise the importance of adequate information and a robust understanding of significance (as required by the NPPF).

Information required

Where piling is being considered as part of a foundation design on a site containing archaeological remains, a range of site-specific information will be needed to meet the standards of understanding set out under the NPPF. This is necessary to enable sound decision taking with regard to the particular technical issues raised by the use of piled foundations.

The applicant will need to provide sufficient information demonstrating an adequate understanding of the significance of the archaeological site and assessment of potential harm to that significance arising from the development. As set out in Historic England guidance on Preserving Archaeological Remains (2016), the state of preservation of archaeological remains may be a key element of their significance.

The NPPF states that local planning authorities (LPAs) should require developers to submit an appropriate desk-based assessment and where necessary, appropriate field evaluation.

In addition to information required to take planning decisions, it is recommended that sufficient geotechnical site investigation (undertaken in accordance with Eurocode 7) has been conducted early in the design process. This ensures that appropriate engineering information is available to allow for a flexible foundation design to reduce the impact on archaeological remains.

Close working and good information exchange between all parties involved in developing a site containing archaeological remains where piling is proposed as a foundation solution is recommended. It is beneficial for the developer, client and architect to have considered foundation options and inform the piling contractors that archaeological remains are present on site before they tender. This ensures that these sub-contractors are adequately aware of these issues and are able to identify foundation solutions which minimise potential harm to the site and its significance.

It is good practice for technical aspects associated with piled foundations to be appropriately assessed. These include but are not necessarily limited to:

- the potential for the particular pile type utilised to damage archaeological deposits. This may include the possibility that drilling fluids and concrete (prior to setting) from bored or augered piles might leach out adjacent to the pile bore.

- the cumulative impact of successive piling on a site resulting in damage to so much of a site that future re-examination would not be worthwhile.

- the potential for piling to change the site hydrology, draining waterlogged deposits.

Risk assessment

Risk assessment forms a conventional tool in the identification, evaluation, avoidance and control of risk. This guidance lays out an approach to assessing risk to the significance of archaeological remains (with the input of appropriate archaeological advice) as a means to select the most appropriate foundation methods and control measures when working on archaeological sites and to justify this choice with appropriate design and avoidance measures.

The process of risk assessment is best commenced at pre-planning stage and continuously updated during design development as new information becomes available such as from desk based research and site investigations. In many cases the risk assessment process will assist in the identification of opportunities to avoid potentially adverse impacts on the significance of archaeological remains.

Archaeological field evaluation (trial trenching) of a sufficient sample of the site is an important part of the risk assessment process. Piling carried out without effective evaluation of the site could lead to piles being inappropriately located, leading to potential loss or damage to archaeological features. In addition to causing additional loss of information, this is also likely to increase the cost to the developer, such as from the need for foundation re-design.

Overall, it is important that sufficient information is provided to all parties at each of the relevant stages of the pre-application and statutory planning processes and throughout the delivery phases. The design of an appropriate foundation strategy will depend on cooperation, close working and open information exchange between the applicant, the local planning authority and their specialist advisers, and the contractor.

Structure of the document

- This introduction has outlined the planning background and the need for adequate information to be assembled to inform planning decisions, so that appropriate foundations can be designed.

- A summary overview follows which highlights the key points from the text.

- Piles, and the main piling types, are covered in Chapter 3. This outlines the piling techniques used to construct foundations. It also sets out the engineering choices and constraints. This should enable readers to consider the appropriateness of each technique within proposed sustainable foundation schemes.

- Chapter 4 summarises the potential impacts of each pile type on archaeological deposits.

- Chapter 5 discusses how the impact of piling on archaeological sites can be appropriately managed, giving a range of design options and solutions. An emphasis is placed on the types of decisions that planning and archaeological officers, developers, and their archaeological consultants need to consider throughout the design and construction process.

- The risk assessment process is described in Chapter 6, which also includes a blank risk assessment form.

- Case studies are provided in Chapter 7 to demonstrate how some of the design solutions have worked in previous situations.

- Supplementary information is given in Chapter 8 detailing past observations of piling impacts and laboratory studies. These provide the evidence-base for pile impacts described in Chapter 4.

2 Overview of key points

2.1 Early involvement and gathering information

- Pile design is best considered early in the development programme and planning process.

- Feasibility studies for foundation re-use are best carried out early on.

- The risk assessment tool is best used to identify the least damaging foundation solution.

- It is good practice for site evaluation and site investigation to be sufficiently detailed so that the impact of piling on all archaeology across the site can be fully understood.

- Site characterisation is likely to be insufficient without a detailed model showing the depth of archaeological deposits.

- Close working between the applicant, the local planning authority and the contractor is recommended from the outset.

- As set out in Historic England advice on **Preserving Archaeological Remains**, following the NPPF, the applicant will need to ensure that they adequately understand and can describe the significance and state of preservation of archaeological materials present and have assessed the harm to that significance arising from the development.

2.2 Pile impact

- New piling impact on the site's archaeological remains is best kept to a minimum.

- The cumulative impact of previous foundations may mean that the impact of new piling will compromise the legibility of the archaeological deposits. Under these circumstances, piling may not offer a viable design solution for preserving the archaeological remains within the development.

- It should be possible to avoid the most archaeologically sensitive areas of the site through careful pile placement and appropriate load-bearing spanning structures.

- Where piles are placed in clusters, the close spacing reduces the future legibility of the enclosed archaeological deposits. Groups of three or more piles and pile cap represent a single area of impact and need to be mitigated accordingly.

2.3 Choosing the right foundation solution

- Piled foundations are typically chosen over shallow foundations eg, footings or rafts because of high loading and settlement performance. But nevertheless, shallow foundations should first be considered, where appropriate, to mitigate impacts on archaeology.

- Using the risk assessment methodology (see Chapter 5), the appropriate pile choice should be made identifying the one that will provide the greatest level of preservation of the archaeological remains on site. The choice will also depend on the engineering requirements of the development and these two will need to be balanced.

- As part of that risk assessment process, the impact of each pile type is assessed by the design team. This impact will vary depending on ground conditions and the type of archaeological deposit. The risk assessment process considers physical impact as well as any impact on the site hydrogeology, chemistry and microbiology.

- The choice of pile solution must also consider the impact of any enabling and temporary works required for a pile solution. These will differ with pile type eg pile probing, piling platform, access to pile locations. For example, the piling platform could be greater than 1 metre thick depending on the ground conditions and size of the piling equipment.

- It is good practice for a thorough archaeological evaluation and characterisation of the site to be undertaken prior to piling to indicate the likelihood of encountering buried structures (either archaeological or modern) which can cause obstructions to piling.

- Where these obstructions cannot be avoided by careful placement of the piles, a methodology for removing or coring through them, forms a key element of the mitigation strategy. In the latter case, a tool capable of cutting through these obstructions should be specified in the risk assessment process and used.

Displacement piles

- Displacement piles may be driven (impact or vibrated) or pressed in. Where displacement piles are used, the area of potential damage is not just restricted to the pile itself, but can impact the adjacent area as well. The area of impact will vary depending on ground conditions and method of installation.

- A general estimation (based on laboratory studies and on-site observations) is that driven displacement piles can damage an area twice the width of the pile cross-section (and so four times the area).

- As the actual zone of effect of a displacement pile may differ, the onus rests with the applicant to demonstrate if they believe the area of impact will be lower than indicated here. Evaluation of previous foundations where they exist on a site will help to establish specific conditions.

- To achieve more certainty about the total area of damage from displacement piles, and to reduce the amount of damage, pile locations can be pre-augered before the pile is installed.

Non-displacement piles

- The area of physical loss is designed to relate purely to the area of the pile, but exceptions occur when the pile bore sides collapse (not likely for CFA piles), or when concrete from the pile migrates into voids or the unconsolidated deposits adjacent to the bored/augered hole. In both cases, these impacts can be mitigated by installing temporary or permanent casing (Figure 1). The impact on fragile deposits such as timber and other structures should be considered.

2.4 Managing construction risks

- Ground investigation, boreholes, test trenches and other invasive work to understand ground conditions for geotechnical purposes will have an archaeological impact. A methodology for such work should be drawn up and agreed by all parties.

- To avoid damage during piling, it is recommended that in addition to the risk assessment document, a detailed methodology for the piling works and enabling works is drawn up and agreed by all parties.

- To ensure that this plan is adhered to, it may be appropriate to maintain an archaeological presence on site during the piling works.

- In addition to damage during pile installation, damage to archaeological remains can also occur during site remediation and from ground clearance work, including pile probing. These activities should be avoided on sites containing archaeological remains; their impact should be assessed using the risk assessment methodology.

Figure 1: Concrete migration into a void, in this case from the pile cap. © University of Leicester Archaeological Services (ULAS)

3   Piling types

Piling is a method of transferring load from a structure into the ground. The engineering objective of a pile is to support a structure by using the strength of the ground some distance below the surface that can resist the imposed force. This can be by direct bearing onto a firm stratum present at depth below the site or by using the frictional resistance of the soil against the pile shaft to develop the load-bearing capacity. In some cases, a combination of these is used where the pile is founded on a firm horizon and the sides develop surface friction (Figures 2 and 3).

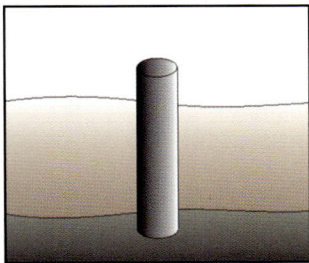

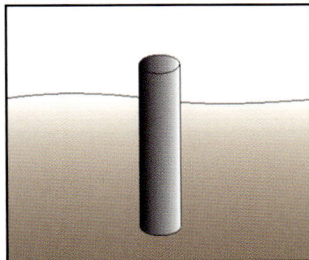

Engineering factors influencing the choice of pile type may include:

■ The proposed building design, structure and location (for example, high-rise urban flats or low-rise greenfield warehousing).

■ Ground conditions (ie cohesive or non-cohesive soil) and location of the water table.

■ Durability (for example, concrete can suffer chemical attack and steel piles may corrode).

■ Cost (including speed of installation and certainty of the chosen method being effective).

Pile types in this guidance note are grouped and described under the headings of displacement and non-displacement piles (see Figure 4).

Figures 2, 3 and 4: End bearing pile, where the pile is founded in the hard incompressible layer rather than the soil above (top). Friction bearing pile, where the sediment becomes increasingly stiff with depth (bottom). Pile types (right).

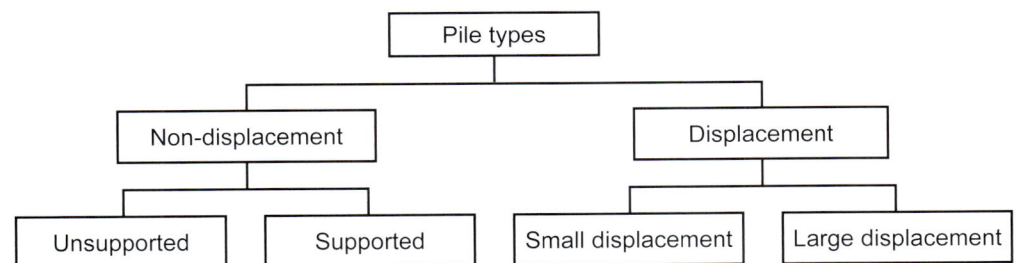

3.1 Displacement piles

Displacement piles push the sediment aside as they are installed, compressing the ground and increasing the resistance of the foundation. Displacement piles are environmentally positive in the sense that there is no need to remove spoil, no landfill requirements, and reduced vehicle movements. This is particularly important on contaminated sites where the arisings (spoil) would require remediation. There are several forms of displacement pile (Figure 5).

Figure 5: Displacement pile types.

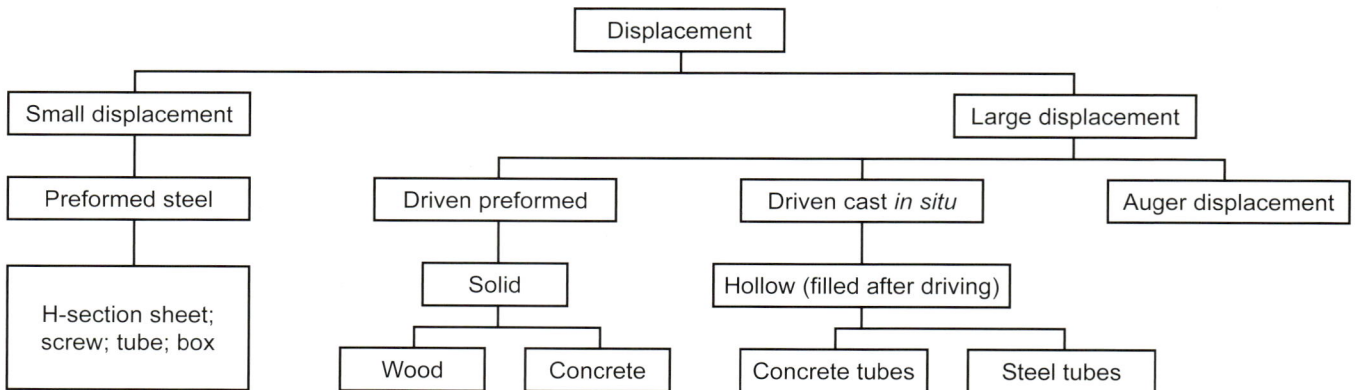

```
                            ┌──────────────┐
                            │ Displacement │
                            └──────────────┘
          ┌───────────────────────┴───────────────────────────────┐
┌────────────────────┐                              ┌──────────────────────┐
│ Small displacement │                              │  Large displacement  │
└────────────────────┘                              └──────────────────────┘
          │                      ┌──────────────────────┼──────────────────────────┐
┌────────────────────┐ ┌──────────────────┐  ┌───────────────────┐   ┌──────────────────────┐
│  Preformed steel   │ │ Driven preformed │  │ Driven cast in situ│   │ Auger displacement   │
└────────────────────┘ └──────────────────┘  └───────────────────┘   └──────────────────────┘
          │                      │                      │
┌────────────────────┐    ┌──────────┐   ┌───────────────────────────┐
│  H-section sheet;  │    │  Solid   │   │ Hollow (filled after driving)│
│  screw; tube; box  │    └──────────┘   └───────────────────────────┘
└────────────────────┘    ┌─────┴─────┐        ┌──────────┴──────────┐
                     ┌─────────┐ ┌──────────┐ ┌────────────────┐ ┌────────────┐
                     │  Wood   │ │ Concrete │ │ Concrete tubes │ │ Steel tubes│
                     └─────────┘ └──────────┘ └────────────────┘ └────────────┘
```

3.2 Large displacement piles

Large displacement piles (enclosed solid element) can be constructed from concrete, metal or, less commonly timber, and are installed by impact (hammering), pressing in (jacking) or vibrating the piles (or tubes) into the ground (Figure 6). Traditionally a drop-hammer would simply drop a large weight onto the top of the pile, however, they can produce significant

Figure 6: Displacement pile installation: Piles arrive at site, pile located, pile section driven, additional section attached, pile driven. © Roger Bullivant Limited

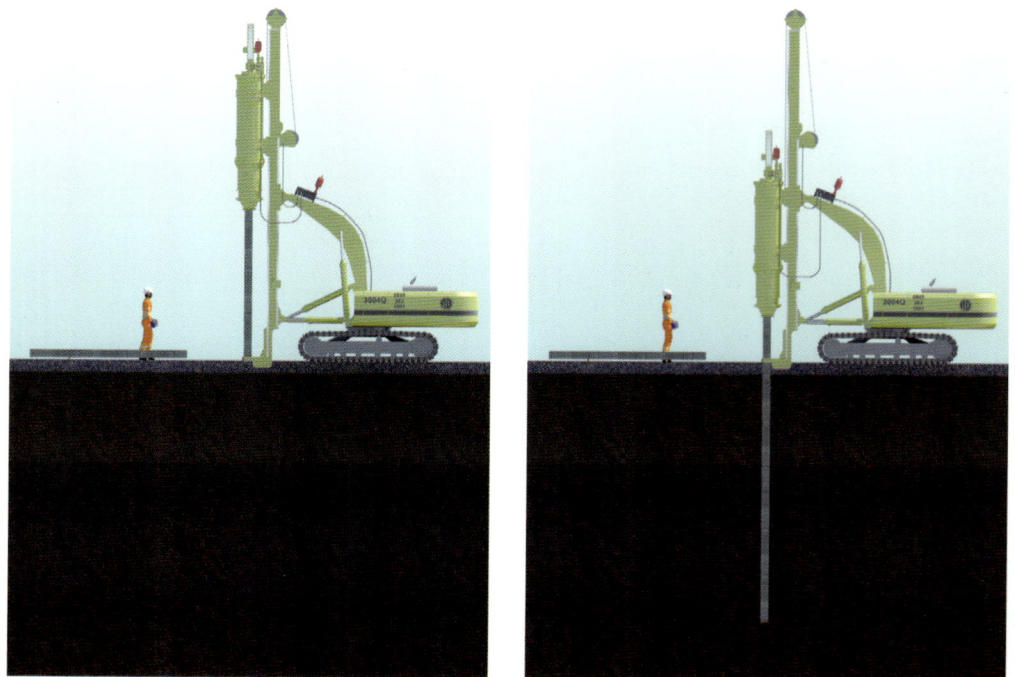

Figure 7: Preformed concrete displacement pile being installed. © Roger Bullivant Limited

noise and vibration (Figure 7 – in this image the hammer is encased which helps to minimise the noise generated). Modern hydraulic hammers use a controllable powered ram and are quieter and cause less vibration than the drop-hammer. To drive or extract a pile by means of inducing a vibration into the pile element, greatly reduces skin friction properties and allows the pile to move through the ground with considerably less resistance than it would do under a static load. Fast rotation, out of balance, cams apply vertical vibration to the pile, liquefying granular solid and facilitating very speedy pile installation. These machines have been refined so that they can jump between frequencies and amplitude to suit the ground whilst avoiding damaging harmonic vibrations which would stress nearby structures. A crane suspended unit allows reach, often beneficial in marine works or areas where piling rig access would be problematic. It can be a lower cost option than a piling rig configuration. If sediments are soft, preformed piles are pressed in (jacked) rather than hammered in, which has the advantage of being quiet and effectively vibration-free.

Driven preformed piles

Solid piles are usually constructed from precast concrete (and occasionally wood) and come as specific lengths or sections joined together on site to form a longer pile, up to c 40m; in Figure 8 pile sections can be seen stored in the background, waiting to be installed. Low headroom rigs can be used in areas of restricted access. The normal range of preformed concrete pile sizes in the UK is 150-300mm diameter. The advantage of using preformed concrete piles is that there is no need to wait for concrete to set, nor for liquid concrete to be transported to, or prepared on, site. The pile sections can be coated before insertion to prevent reaction with the surrounding soil, improve concrete durability and/or to reduce friction with the ground during installation.

Figure 8: Installing sections of a preformed concrete pile. © Roger Bullivant Limited

Hollow piles are tubes generally constructed of steel or occasionally precast concrete. The concrete may be pre-stressed to enhance durability. Hollow piles are often used when large diameters (>500mm) are needed and are hollow for ease of handling, or for economy. For hollow steel piles, concrete is poured into the hollow section to complete the pile (as for driven cast *in situ*), except that in this case the tubes are not withdrawn.

Driven cast *in situ*

This method is used less often than driven precast piles. A tube (steel or precast concrete) with a sacrificial shoe or detachable point is driven into the ground, displacing and compacting the soil around the tube. Reinforcement is lowered into the tube and concrete poured into it. As the concrete is added, the tube is withdrawn and the concrete may be compacted. This method is normally used to create piles from about 250-500mm diameter with depths of up to 25m.

This method is particularly useful in contaminated soils, because no arisings are produced; however, removal of the tube can cause distortion of the surrounding sediment and may allow movement of liquid concrete into voids.

Auger displacement piles

This method uses a spiral auger that displaces the spoil laterally into the ground around the hole. Concrete is poured down the auger shaft as the auger is withdrawn, see Figures 9 and 10. The displacement consolidates the ground surrounding the pile, resulting in enhanced soil properties and therefore shorter pile lengths.

Pile sizes will depend on the individual pile company's specific auger design, but diameters of 300mm to 600mm are likely. This type of pile is relatively 'green', its installation producing very little spoil, vibration and noise.

Figures 9 and 10: Construction process for auger displacement piles (left). Auger displacement pile rig, note tapered auger head (right). Both images © Cementation Skanska

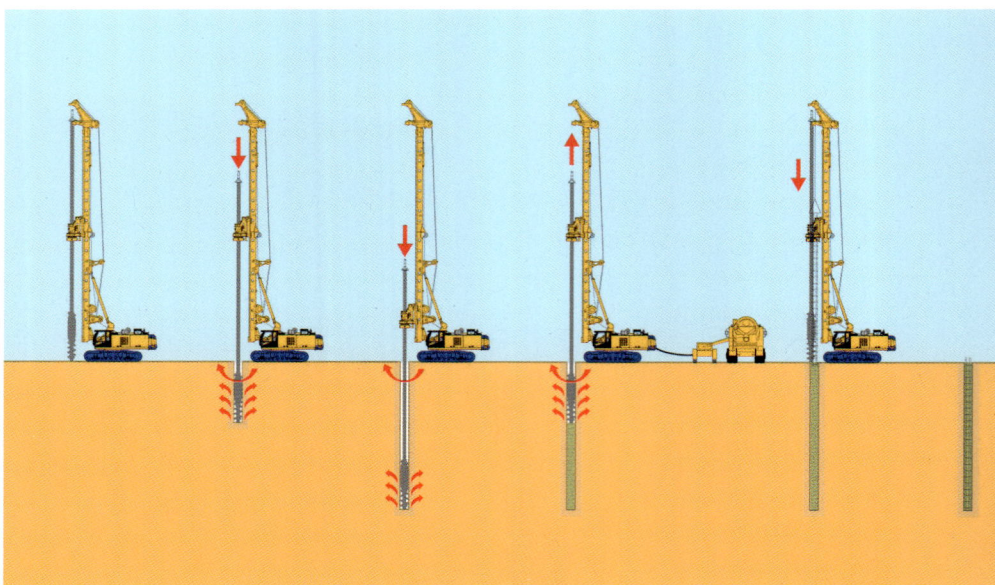

3.3 Small displacement piles

Driven preformed steel

Small driven displacement piles are typically steel sections (H-section, sheet, tube or box) are either hammered (impact) or vibrated into the ground. Sheet piles (Figure 11) are often constructed as interlocking piles, used to create cofferdams or retaining walls, and less often to support load from a structure above. Where they are used for retaining walls, sheet piles may also need tie-backs, which will have a further impact on adjacent deposits. Small displacement piles can also be extracted by means of vibration or jacking.

Figures 11 and 12: Sheet pile retaining wall along the edge of a site at Drapers' Gardens (left) © Pre-Construct Archaeology Ltd. Rolled steel tube being installed at Skirbeck Road, Boston (right).

Steel pile installation is covered in detail in guidance provided by the Steel Piling Group (2018).

Smaller metal piles include rolled steel sections (see Figure 12), screw piles and H-section piles. Rolled steel section piles are easily handled and can be driven hard, and in very long lengths; while the pile length can be readily varied, lengths of up to 36m can be achieved.

Press in preformed steel

Pressing in of preformed steel piles (typically sheet piles or tubes) by hydraulic pushing has brought noise and vibration to minimal levels. The installation plant can walk on the top of a line of piles and hence install in restricted access areas which were previously impossible (eg over water or soft ground) without the need of a piling platform. Where driving is very difficult a pre-bore auger or high-pressure water jet can be attached to locally disturb the ground ahead of the toe.

Steel screw piles

Screw piles (eg helical piles), for lightly loaded structures, are often of modular configuration, often consisting of a number of connected tubes 2-3m with a series of steel plates welded to the tubes (see **case study 7.2 for an example of their use on an archaeologically sensitive site**). Due to installation constraints, lengths are often limited to 12-15m but may be less depending on ground conditions. Steel piles are liable to corrosion, which can be treated using cathodic protection, or a pile coating.

Engineering advantages and disadvantages of displacement piles

The advantages of displacement piles lie in the range of installation methods available, their preformed construction and the controlled and clean nature of the installation. They are also extractable. Very limited volumes of spoil are produced and piles are generally preformed with no need to transport or make fresh concrete on site, except when casting *in situ*. Piles can be quickly constructed in variable and long lengths, (also in low-headroom areas) and are unaffected by the presence of groundwater. Additionally, off-site production in controlled conditions means the preformed sections are constructed to a higher and more uniform specification than is possible with on-site piles cast *in situ*. In general, small driven piles and metal screw piles are particularly useful if ground displacements and disturbance must be curtailed.

Disadvantages with displacement piles include breakage below ground, and the difficulties of checking pile quality. Soil displacement can cause heave, and lift or damage adjacent piles or damage adjacent buildings. The noise and vibration associated with pile installation can be considerable, and can make this method unsuitable in built-up areas and adjacent to fragile historic structures.

3.4 Non-displacement (bored) piles

Non-displacement piles (Figure 13) are installed by boring a hole, removing the arisings and filling the hole with concrete (and often reinforcement). The bore tends to consist of a screw-type auger on a piling rig, which augers directly into the ground and removes arisings in a series of passes, using a 'flighted' or bucket auger (see Figure 14). Piles are usually cast *in situ* or occasionally constructed using pre-cast concrete ring sections, which are then filled with concrete. Piles can be constructed with diameters of up to 3m, and can be bored to depths of up to 70m, with under-reamed bases up to three times the shaft size. Small diameter bored piles are usually less than 600mm diameter and can reach 30m in most ground conditions. Bored micro-piles are of the order of 200-300mm in diameter and reach up to 30m deep and are particularly capable of penetrating obstructions due to the wide variety of drilling techniques available, such as high-speed rotation, drilling bits etc.

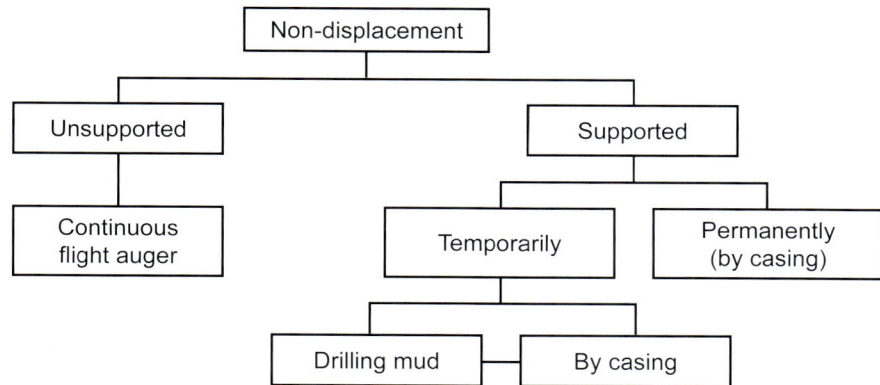

Figure 13: Non-displacement pile types.

In some instances a casing is inserted, usual.y temporarily, to prevent the collapse of the hole, and the auger drills inside this (shown in Figure 14). In the case of continuous flight-augered (CFA) piles, the arisings are removed at the end of the operation when the auger is removed, making support unnecessary. With any of these non-displacement piling methods, there is typically little or no sediment displacement adjacent to the shaft of the pile. Increased pile capacities can be achieved through the formation of enlarged pile bases (under-reams).

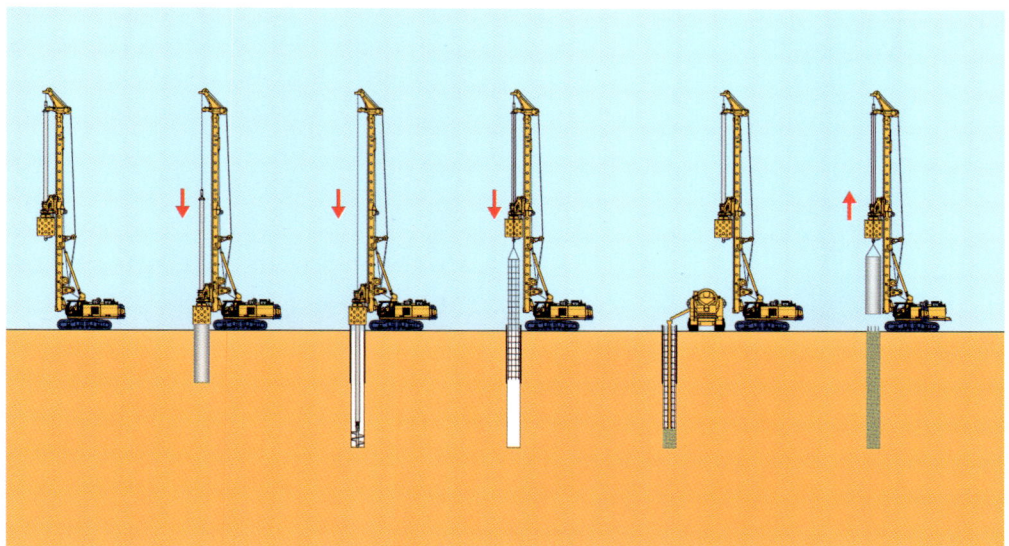

Figure 14: Illustration of rotary bored pile construction. A temporary casing is installed to prevent the upper deposits collapsing, The auger is advanced and soil removed, the reinforcement and concrete are added, the casing is removed and the pile is complete.
© Cementation Foundations Skanska

3.5   Supported non-displacement (bored) piles

In unstable soils a casing or a support fluid, such as bentonite/polymer, may be used to temporarily support the pile bore. The choice between using steel casing or support fluid is an engineering decision; generally casings are used to line a relatively shallow depth of unstable ground to reach a self-supporting stratum below, while a support fluid is used to temporarily support the pile bore at deeper depths.

Temporarily supported

A support fluid would be used when piling through a deep, unstable stratum and subsequently pumped out. The use of support fluid has specific implications, including adverse environmental effects and the large space required for support fluid plant and storage on site. Bentonite support fluids may be classified as controlled waste, in which case disposal requires special precautions and additional expense.

Pile casings are generally steel tubes inserted into the ground by driving, vibration, oscillation or rotation. Noise and ground vibration can be high where a casing is installed. These levels, however, will generally be much less than for driven pile installation, although tripod-bored piles can also produce significant noise and vibration. Casings are also installed by pre-boring an open hole or 'mudding in', the contact between the casing and soil being lubricated using support fluid. This can significantly reduce the noise and vibration effects.

Casing is typically not installed through obstructions. However, where advance obstruction removal is not feasible or there are extensive or deep obstructions temporary thick wall casing can core through most obstructions. Where archaeological deposits contain significant voids, casing can be used to mitigate concrete migration. However, on temporary casing extraction, some concrete migration may occur. Most casings are removed after the pile has been formed, although some are left in place permanently, even though this adds significantly to the cost.

3.6   Unsupported non-displacement continuous flight auger (CFA) piles

The CFA technique is one of the most common piling forms and can be used in most soils. The auger is screwed into the ground to the specified depth and high slump concrete is then pumped down the auger stem to the base (see Figures 15-17).

As the concrete is inserted, the auger is withdrawn, taking the arisings with it. A reinforcing cage can then be pushed into the liquid concrete. Limited vibration or noise is generated using this piling technique. Pile diameters are usually 0.3-1.2m and they can reach depths of 30m. Casing is rarely needed as the sides of the bore do not need supporting as the arisings are not removed until the concrete is pumped in. The cased CFA technique, where the auger is advanced together with temporary casing, may be employed when having to penetrate a known obstruction or hard ground, or when constructing secant piled walls.

Engineering advantages and disadvantages of non-displacement piling

The benefits of using non-displacement piles include the variability of length and diameter, the low risk of ground heave resulting from pile installation, and the low noise and vibration.

Disadvantages include the need to bring liquid concrete to site, or create concrete/support fluid plant on site. A further disadvantage is that CFA piles cannot be inspected once cast. For bored piles where a support fluid has not been used, the open pile bore can be inspected before placing of concrete, so the length, depth, shaft, and base quality and verticality can be easily verified. Support fluid or casings are usually required to construct bored piles

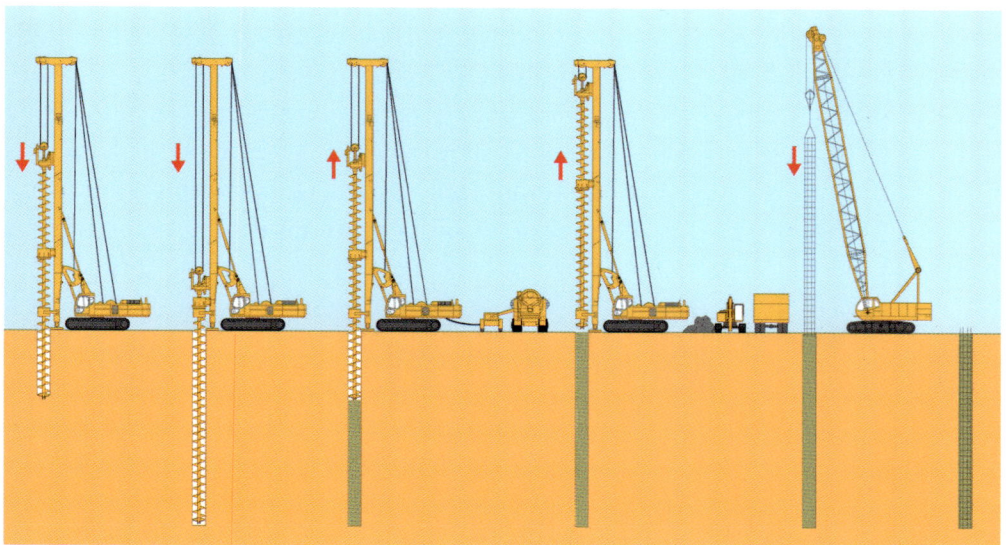

Figure 15: Photograph from above a CFA pile during the construction of a pile. Soil can be seen in the lower flights, and around the auger where it has been cleaned off. The reinforcement cage stands adjacent (left). © Cementation Foundations Skanska

Figure 16: Illustration of CFA pile construction: The auger is located and rotated into the ground to the desired depth, as it is withdrawn the concrete is added, and finally reinforcement is added and the pile is complete. © Cementation Foundations Skanska

Figure 17: Continuous Flight Auger (CFA) piling. © Cementation Foundations Skanska

in unstable sediments and the transport, use, storage and disposal of these materials and fluids all need to be taken into account. Site establishment of plant, materials, access and working platforms can be more extensive than displacement piles.

3.7 Pile retaining walls

Bored concrete pile retaining walls are created by drilling a line of holes and forming piles either as contiguous (adjacent) or interlocking (secant) sections (Figure 18). Secant walls are drilled in two phases – primary piles, then secondary piles that partly cut the primary piles. They are often used to retain the surrounding ground as well as for their high stiffness and water-retaining properties. Contiguous pile walls will not retain water but are cheaper than secant walls. These types of pile are generally between 0.45m and 3.0m in diameter and can reach lengths of 60m. In virtually all cases guide trenches are constructed before secant (but not necessarily contiguous) walls are created in order to remove obstructions and create the line. This will therefore remove soil, which might then need to be taken from site. Pile retaining walls are not always used to support a building, but to contain lateral stress, for example within basements.

Retaining walls can also be formed by interlocking preformed steel sections eg steel sheet pile (see Section 3.3). Further information on pile retaining walls is given in the Institution of Civil Engineers Manual of Geotechnical Engineering Volume II (Burland et al 2012).

Figure 18: Secant pile wall in background, from Gresham Street, London. © MOLA

3.8   Vibro ground improvement techniques

In soft or loose ground conditions, ground improvement techniques (commonly using vibration) are sometimes used instead of piling to form foundations. However, from the archaeologist's point of view, vibro methods present similar problems and so are briefly considered here. They use densification and/or the insertion of stone or concrete columns to provide greater below-ground stability prior to construction. Key techniques are vibro compaction and the creation of columns using displacement and non-displacement methods, such as vibro replacement (Mitchell and Jardine 2002). Dynamic compaction involves dropping a large weight onto the ground and should not be confused with vibro compaction.

Vibro compaction and vibro replacement – stone columns

Vibro replacement methods are used in mixed cohesive, granular or purely cohesive soils, particularly weak soils and fill. A vibrating poker is used to create a hole into which stone aggregate is inserted and vibrated to bond with the surrounding soil. Vibro compaction is rarely used in the UK; it requires purely granular soils with low silt content. Vibro compaction uses a vibrating poker (often 300-400mm diameter), inserted into granular soils to agitate and compact them; water is often used with this system to remove very fine particles and assist in penetration (Figure 19).

Vibro concrete columns [VCC]

Concrete columns [VCC] can also be constructed using vibro techniques. A vibrating poker creates a void, usually through weak soils and is founded on a solid layer. Once the void is created by horizontally and vertically displacing the soil, a very low slump concrete is pumped into the hole through the poker (Figures 20 and 21).

Engineering advantages and disadvantages of ground improvement techniques

As columns of stone or concrete are inserted to create a support grid within the soil, this increases ground-bearing capacity without generating spoil and so is considered environmentally sustainable. Additionally, although 'stone' columns are often aggregate, recycled ballast is now regularly used, furthering sustainable development. A high-density grid of vibro columns is particularly useful where increased load-bearing is required. When stone columns are used as foundations (rather than for ground stabilisation), more columns are usually required than piles.

1 With the vibrocat stabilised on hydraulic outriggers, the leaders are elevated to the vertical and the vibrator located on the ground at the stone column position. The skip is charged with stone.

2 The skip travels up the leaders and automatically discharges stone into the reception chamber at the top of the vibrator.

3 The vibrator penetrates the weak soils to the design depth under the action of the vibrations, compressed air and pull-down winch facility.

4 At the required depth, stone is released and compacted by small upward and downward movements of the vibrator, the pull-down being employed on the downward compacting action.

5 With stone being added to the system as necessary at any stage of the construction procedure, a stone column of very high integrity, tightly interlocked with the surrounding soil, is built up to ground level.

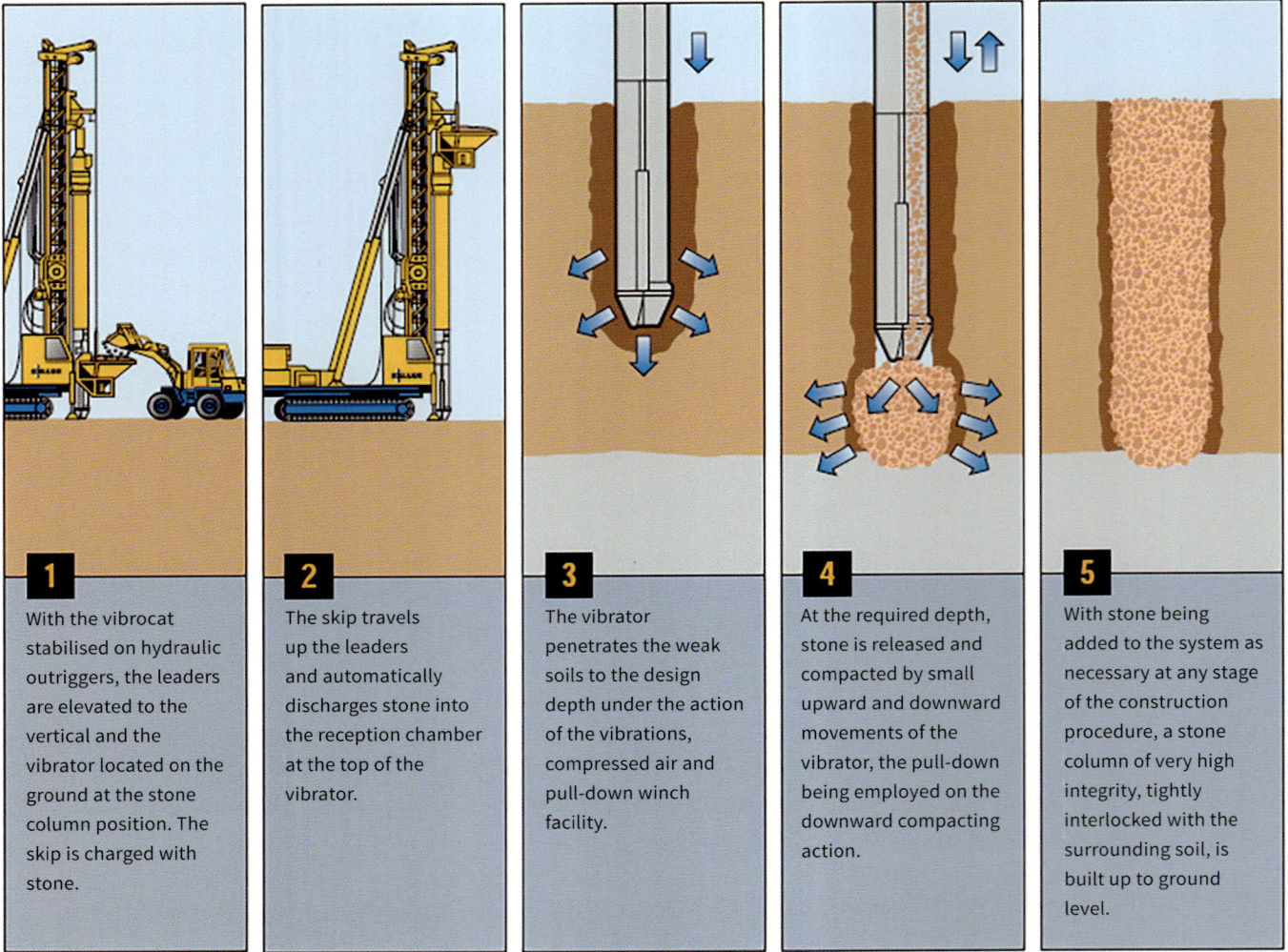

Figures 19, 20, 21:
Bottom feed vibro
replacement. © Keller
Ground Engineering

4 Piling impacts upon archaeological remains

In this section, the impact of each of the pile types is explored, detailing physical and hydrogeological impacts upon archaeological remains. All piling techniques result in damage to or loss of artefacts and sediment deformation equal to at least the total volume of the pile or vibro-replaced column. This is the minimum impact that will result from any piling operation. In many cases, further disturbance may occur, and the extent of that disturbance must be understood in order that the impact and implications of foundations and piling schemes can be assessed. Additionally, hydrogeological impacts on the deposits may affect the deposit/groundwater chemistry. This is not only relevant on waterlogged sites, as changes in deposit hydrogeology and chemistry can affect inorganic as well as organic remains.

Unintended damage to archaeological remains can also occur during other elements of the construction programme, such as during demolition / site clearance / site investigation, or as part of enabling works; in the removal of obstacles to piling (often called pile probing); and from vehicle movements and loading from those vehicles (including piling rigs).

4.1 Large displacement pile impacts

Driven preformed piles: physical impacts

During pile installation, sediment is physically displaced vertically and horizontally, which can cause distortion and damage to archaeological deposits, structures and artefacts. The effects of this have been recorded in excavations adjacent to previous piles (see for example Figure 22) and from model scale laboratory studies. Details of these are given in Chapter 8. The level of impact depends on the pile type and deposits, but as a general rule of thumb, physical impacts from driven preformed piles occur within 1.5 pile widths of the pile centreline. However, in several cases the area of damage is less.

Figure 22: Damage to human remains caused by piling. © University of Leicester Archaeological Services (ULAS)

As driven preformed piles are constructed off-site, the potential impact on deposit hydrogeology and geochemistry is likely to be less than where the pile is cast *in situ*. The compression of deposits adjacent to the pile should lead to a reduction in permeability in this area, thereby reducing hydraulic conductivity of sediments at the soil/pile interface. However, where piling occurs through perched water-tables, there is a potential for dragged down and deformed deposits to create a pathway for downward migration of water, resulting in the dewatering of previously waterlogged deposits. From model scale research, this seems to be a greater risk with H-section piles.

Driven cast *in situ* piles: impacts

The physical impact of driven cast *in situ* piles is similar to driven piles, that is, vertical and horizontal displacement of deposits up to 1.5 pile widths from the pile centreline. It is possible that further modification of deposits occurs when the casing is removed. Currently, there has been no evaluation of this, so caution should be applied in assessing the likely damage using this technique. Aside from the physical impact associated with the removal of the tubing, if the pile grout is still liquid it could escape into any voids. These voids might be present in poorly consolidated deposits, or perhaps in fissures within the sediment. In waterlogged deposits there is a risk that chemical interaction will occur between the pile grout and archaeological remains. This is discussed in more detail within the section on non-displacement (bored) piles below.

Screw displacement piles: impacts

Limited evidence exists about the physical impacts on archaeological remains from screw displacement augers. This technique may be more damaging than non-displacement piling, because the displacement auger forces the sediment aside, leading to sediment deformation in the vicinity of the pile. The sediment adjacent to the pile will have been compacted, decreasing permeability at the soil/pile interface, relative to a non-displacement pile. Therefore, potential impacts, discussed in more detail for non-displacement piles, such as grout migration are less likely to occur. However, this is an area where further research is needed to characterise the nature of below-ground soil movement. It would not be good practice for screw displacement piles to be used as a foundation solution on an archaeological site without a full impact and risk assessment to gain a firm understanding of the likely zone of deformation.

4.2   Small displacement pile impacts

Preformed steel

H-section piles have a smaller cross-sectional area, and therefore, in theory, should lead to less sediment displacement than square preformed driven piles. Although no field investigations have confirmed this, model-scale analysis has shown that there is a reduction in the amount of vertical deformation of deposits. However, the geometry of H-section piles might increase the potential for liquid movement along the pile, which is discussed further in Chapter 8.

Sheet piles also have a limited cross-sectional area and the amount of material displaced during installation will be significantly lower than other pile types. Sediment deformation is therefore most likely to occur where obstructions are encountered, and archaeological material is dragged down, or the original orientation of materials is altered. In many cases though, sheet piling will cut through archaeological materials. The installation techniques used for sheet piling, including impact and vibro driving can induce ground vibrations that might damage fragile archaeological materials or adjacent buildings.

Where sheet piles are used to create an impermeable barrier (such as a cofferdam), then de-watering may occur. One study carried out in Bergen, Norway, has shown that substantial water flow occurred through a small hole in the sheet pile (Matthiesen 2005). An investigation of the state of preservation of material on either side of the sheet piling indicated that there was no significant difference. The potential risks from dewatering will depend on the true level of permeability of any given barrier and the specific hydrogeological circumstances of any given site.

Figure 23: Small screw piles in advance of installation in Salisbury (see case study 7.2). © Tim Sheward

Steel screw piles (see Figure 23) are likely to have minimal physical impact on archaeological deposits (where obstructions are avoided) and have the added benefit that they can be unscrewed when they are no longer required, a process that should also involve little damage to deposits. The main impact will be the displacement of material during insertion. Additionally, if obstructions become caught between the pile blades, then this could lead to further disturbance. Since some compaction of the ground adjacent to the pile will occur, the pile is unlikely to act as a major conduit for migration of water or contamination within archaeological deposits. There is potential for corrosion of the pile above the groundwater table. This may have an impact at the time of pile removal if corrosion products have become integrated with the surrounding soil or archaeological material, which may lead to greater disturbance as the pile is removed.

4.3 Supported non-displacement (bored) pile impacts

Temporarily supported bore: physical impacts

An accepted impact associated with conventional bored piles is the loss of material from within the cross-section of the bore. In principle, the boring should not disturb material adjacent to the hole, but this is negated if the auger encounters obstructions (eg timber, concrete, masonry, cobbles, boulders) that are forced outward or dragged down through significant deposits outside the intended bore.

Few published examples exist where archaeological evaluations recorded details of previously installed non-displacement piles and this is an area where further field observations are needed.

During the installation of temporary or permanent casing vibration may occur, and the impact of this, in addition to that of the installation and removal of the casing, has not been fully evaluated. There is a potential risk, highlighted by Nixon (1998), that the installation and removal of the casing may damage an area greater than the diameter of the casing itself. As temporary casings are usually installed to support poorly consolidated deposits, this should reduce any collapse of the bore walls or migration of pile grout into sediment voids. These concerns should be identified in the risk assessment process and discussed by archaeologists and piling engineers on a site-by-site basis.

Other physical impacts may occur where stone, timber and other materials are not cleanly severed by the bore or casing and are pushed aside or dragged down (Nixon 1998, 41). It is possible to get borers capable of cutting through brick and soft stone and it is essential that the likelihood of encountering such sub-surface ground obstacles is clearly addressed in the risk assessment and piling method statement; unforeseen obstructions may hold up the construction programme, and necessitate excavation to remove them. This excavation can be exceptionally damaging to archaeological deposits, and can mean that much a greater area of the site is affected than just the pile locations.

Where bentonite (or synthetic polymer) is used to support unstable sediments, consideration should be given to the impact of this on archaeological deposits. The complexity of the operation means that a compound often needs to be constructed on site for the slurry processing plant. Bentonite is inert so it should pose no chemical risks to archaeological deposits. There may still be physical impact from the use of bentonite which need to be considered within the risk assessment process. For example, where the site is likely to contain voids or the archaeological deposits are poorly consolidated, there is an enhanced risk of the slurry entering these areas. In these cases, a temporary casing could be used for the depth of the archaeologically sensitive deposits.

Temporarily supported bore: hydrogeological impacts

There is a potential risk that the introduction of an alkaline mixture (concrete) will damage archaeological deposits, particularly waterlogged ones. Concrete curing is exothermic (Davis *et al* 2004), the heat potentially acting as a catalyst for further reactions (see Edwards 1998). The potential for mixing of grout and groundwater and for transport of alkaline solution across a greater proportion of the site has yet to be fully evaluated. Where concrete cures quickly and bonds with the sediment of the bore wall, permeability and the potential for transport of alkali materials from the concrete in the groundwater should be reduced. This is a topic where more research is

Figure 24: Borehole rig with CFA piling rig in the background, during sample retrieval to investigate pile cement migration. © Mark Allen

needed (for example as shown in Figure 24), particularly in places where the hydraulic conductivity of the deposits is high, and the movement of groundwater is therefore fast. Further consideration of these theoretical risks is given in Section 5.8.

4.4   Unsupported non-displacement CFA pile impacts

Continuous flight auger (CFA): physical impacts

With CFA piling the auger is screwed into the ground so that the auger provides temporary support for the pile bore. Upon reaching pile depth concrete is injected through the base of the auger whilst the auger is withdrawn. All of this significantly reduces the potential of pile wall collapse. If the auger is rotated too rapidly then adjacent material may be drawn into the bore (called flighting). Flighting is undesirable and will tend to occur when the auger penetrates a harder stratum beneath a soft or loose stratum or due to poor construction control. Flighting can be avoided by good construction control, using a cased-CFA or other piling method.

Provided the auger is advanced at the right speed, and obstructions are not encountered, CFA piling should not physically damage deposits outside the area of the auger.

Where archaeological deposits contain structural material (bricks, stone, wood) then these obstructions may be dragged within the auger flights and damage adjacent deposits. Structural remains can be displaced if the surrounding ground is too weak to restrict their movement or where a suitable cutting head has not been used. Observations of non-displacement pile impacts in The Netherlands verify these conclusions with the greatest levels of damage occurring to walls and floors. Pile probing to identify and clear possible below ground obstructions in advance of CFA piles can also cause significant damage (see **pile probing**).

A further risk with CFA piles is that concrete may migrate into any voids adjacent to the bore. Any hydrogeological and geochemical impacts will be similar to those discussed for supported non-displacement piles (above).

4.5   Vibro ground improvement techniques

Vibro replacement: physical impacts

One of the principal disadvantages of vibro replacement is that material is forced into the ground, displacing sediment (and archaeological deposits). As the process involves vibration, the soil adjacent to the column is considerably disturbed during the displacement process and this is likely to have a very significant impact on adjacent archaeological deposits. Furthermore, columns are usually installed at around 1.5m to 3.0m c/c (column centres) so there tend to be more replacement columns on a site than if it were piled, increasing the frequency of any impacts. However, there have been few opportunities for archaeologists to evaluate the effects of ground improvement techniques so at present the impacts are not fully understood. The onus should rest with those proposing to use this technique on an archaeological site to clearly demonstrate the harm to significance that it will cause. If the harm is perceived to be too high, then these techniques are unlikely to be a useful way to preserve the archaeological remains on the site.

Vibro compaction and vibro replacement: hydrogeological impacts

Where vibro replacement stone columns are constructed, although these are extremely dense, there is a potential that they could act as conduits for the movement of contaminants, moisture and fluids. In such conditions a concrete plug is generally installed to avoid the dispersion of contaminants. Where the hole created by the vibrating poker is filled with concrete rather than stone, the potential for grout migration will be very limited, as any voids are likely to have been consolidated by the initial vibration. Given the extent to which the physical impacts from vibration may have disturbed any adjacent archaeological deposits, consideration of hydrological impacts may be of limited consequence.

4.6 Summary of pile impacts on archaeological deposits and artefacts

Table 1 contains a summary of the information outlined above. Methods to reduce and manage these impacts are given in Section 5, below.

Pile Type	Lateral Sediment displacement	Concrete migration	Creation of preferential pathway	Vibration (noise and sediment movement)	Metal Corrosion (of piles)
Displacement piles (large and small)	Yes	No (although possibly for Driven in cast *in situ* piles)	Not usually, except thinly layered ground and with H-section piles	Yes, can be reduced	Yes with steel sheet and H-section
Auger displacement piles	Yes	Low potential	Low potential	Limited	No
Non-displacement piles	Low potential	Moderate potential, reduced by casing (except for CFA)	Low potential	Limited, but more likely where casing is used	No
Vibro compaction and vibro replacement – stone	Yes	No	Low potential	Yes	No
Vibro replacement – concrete	Yes	Low potential	Low potential	Yes	No

Table 1: Summary of pile impacts

Unfortunately, in England, there has been no clear requirement for archaeologists to collect piling data from redevelopment sites in any rigorous way. In many instances, evaluations have consciously avoided areas adjacent to piles because they are likely to be disturbed (Davies 2004). This results in vital opportunities to understand the past impacts of construction being missed. It is good practice for this to be a basic requirement on any excavation where previous foundations are encountered because it provides a better understanding of site conditions and the likely future potential impacts of proposed new piles.

4.7 Additional key considerations

Vibration

Vibration from piling can affect above-ground structures as well as below-ground archaeological deposits (Figure 25). The issue of vibration from piling in relation to above ground structures is covered in the British Standard (BS) 5228-2 (2009), BS 7385-1 (1990) and BS 7385-2 (1993). The potential impact will be affected by the type of foundation, underlying ground conditions, the building construction and the state of repair of the building (BS 2009: 37).

Figure 25: During pile installation adjacent to the Scheduled Monument of Hussey Tower, Boston, vibration monitors were used to ensure that vibration did not exceed the agreed limits. The pile locations were pre-augered in part to reduce ground vibration.

Although it is noted in BS 7385-2 that "ruins and near ruins" and a number of other constructions of "historical importance" have a lower resistance to vibration and lower tolerance of vibration effects, BS 5228-2 also notes that "a building of historical value should not (unless it is structurally unsound) be assumed to be more sensitive" (1990: 39). Information is also given in BS 5228-2 on how to reduce the impact of vibration from piling; an appendix gives summary case history data on vibration levels measured on site for a range of piling and ground improvement techniques, for a range of deposit types and buildings, including listed buildings.

Further detailed information on vibration from piling on above-ground historic structures is provided in a CIRIA technical note TN142 (Head and Jardine 1992). It summarises a number of other country codes, including the German DIN 4150, as well as Swiss and Swedish standards and codes. The simplest guidance is given below (Table 2), after DIN 4150 (1970) and provides levels of vibration for specific types of buildings.

Category	Type of structure	Permissible pvv (mm/s)
I	Ruins and damaged buildings, protected as monuments	2
II	Buildings with visible defects, cracks in masonry	4
III	Undamaged buildings in technically good condition	8
IV	Well-stiffened buildings (ie industrial)	10-40

Table 2: Permissible peak particle velocity (ppv) for different structures.

For structural monuments, particularly those in less than prime condition, category I (and possibly II) are relevant. Historic buildings, which are built to different specifications than modern well-stiffened buildings should be covered by categories II and III. If vibration from piling is likely to be an issue on site, a more detailed assessment should be made, considering frequency of vibration, ground conditions and the type of building and its foundations (see Head and Jardine 1992, 41-6).

Vibration can also affect archaeological materials below ground, and intense vibration through soil can damage stratigraphy and embedded artefacts (Sidell *et al* 2004). This can be caused by pile installation, dynamic pile testing, and ground improvement techniques such as vibro compaction. Additionally, vibro piling hammers generate high amplitude vibrations during start-up and close-down. The vibrations from the pile travel both laterally and vertically (Figure 26).

Figure 26: Vibration recording during driven piling using geophones, as part of the NERC Urgent project (see Sidell et al 2004).

Piling equipment

Piling equipment includes piling rigs, cranes, auxiliary tracked plant (eg pumps and power packs) and concrete trucks. Large piling rigs can weigh up to 200 tonnes and significantly increase the stresses in the underlying ground and on any buried archaeological remains. Although small piling rigs can exert high bearing pressures, these tend to be concentrated and dissipate quickly with depth. All piling rigs and cranes require a stable piling platform to operate upon and the thickness of this will also surcharge the ground.

Pile size and geometry

Piling requirements on individual sites will relate directly to the structural needs of the building, and the strength and compressibility of the below ground deposits. Since soils behave differently it is difficult to generalise about ground conditions, or specific pile design. For that reason it is not possible to produce simple tables that compare pile type, pile size and zone of impact on archaeological deposits as such tables be misleading. For example, some non-displacement piles may have a lower loading capacity than driven preformed piles of a similar diameter or width, and thereby require more piles to carry a similar load.

Conversely, the installation of preformed driven piles may have a greater impact on these archaeological deposits, with a zone of disturbance at least one pile-width either side of the pile centreline. In cases where it is possible to use a large single bored pile, multiple driven piles (connected by a pile cap) would usually be needed to provide the same load-bearing capacity. Such close grouping of piles makes it more difficult to interpret the intervening deposits, making the effective impact equal to or larger than that of the single bored pile (*see below*, Pile Groups). This underlines the importance of assessing all of these options within the risk assessment framework.

Pile groups

The pile impacts identified above are principally concerned with damage caused by individual piles. However, driven or mini / micro-bored piles are less usually installed as single piles when supporting large structures. Instead, they are grouped and joined by pile caps, which tie into other building elements (Figure 27).

In most cases isolated piles are likely to be less damaging to the site than grouped piles. This is because the area of sediment enclosed within a pile group, for example three or four piles with a triangular or square arrangement, will be more disturbed. It will be more difficult to interpret the site should it be re-excavated, because it can be hard to access small areas of archaeological deposits within a cluster.

These problems are likely to be exacerbated by the use of driven piles where deposits are modified through down-dragging of sediments. Additionally, any potential hydrogeological and geochemical impacts may be greater in areas where piles are more closely spaced. Where used, pile groups could be located in parts of the site that are not archaeologically sensitive, thereby reducing the harm to significance caused by piling.

Pile caps and ground beams

Figure 27: Pile group (see concrete piles in bottom left of image) installed by chance adjacent to archaeological deposits. If the pile group had been placed slightly closer to these hypocaust *pilae*, they would have been more highly damaged, and would have been difficult to fully interpret. © University of Leicester Archaeological Services (ULAS)

Piled foundations do not generally exist in isolation and the presence of pile caps, ground beams and other structural elements needs to be taken into account. Pile caps are generally concrete slabs at the top of the pile, larger than the pile itself and often spanning several piles grouped together. Ground beams are used to connect two or more piles. Their area and depth depends on the distance between piles and where large distances are spanned, the ground beam can be deep and have a significant impact on archaeological deposits. The depth of the existing building slab, and the depth and level of the new basement slab needs to be considered in assessing the impact of ground beams and foundation design. In combination with other foundations, ground beams can be used to span or cantilever over archaeological features allowing piles to be located away from archaeologically sensitive areas. Depending on the use of the building space (including basement requirements), it may be possible to form ground beams within the ground floor slab, so reducing the below ground impact.

Pile testing

To verify the performance of a pile, pile testing is sometimes undertaken prior to and/or during the main pile installation phase. This may require additional piles to be installed. The most common form of test is the 'static' pile test. Methods include applying a known load to the head of the pile and monitoring its settlement, or advancing the pile into the ground at a known rate and measuring the resisting load. In either case a hydraulic jack is required to apply load to the top of the pile. In turn this needs to jack against some form of rigid structure to provide reaction for the test (Figure 28). Two types of reaction are used, the simpler involving large heavy masses such as concrete or steel weights, which are placed above the test pile. The mass used is often referred to as kentledge. The other method of providing reaction is by means of installing two to more additional piles (reaction piles) around the test pile. Steel beams are then attached to the reaction piles such that they run over the test pile and provide reaction for jacking. Possible impacts on archaeological remains from using kentledge as reaction result from the high near-surface ground loads, which may pose a threat to shallow buried remains. Reaction piles will usually result in additional disturbance unless they form part of the foundation design (*see* below).

Figure 28: Static load test. © Cementation Foundations Skanska

Alternative methods of pile testing do not require additional reaction piles to be installed. The most common forms are dynamic (Figure 29) and 'Statnamic' pile tests (Figure 30). Dynamic pile tests are best suited to driven piles and may be undertaken during the installation phase with no additional plant requirements. Statnamic pile testing does require the mobilisation

Figures 29 and 30: Monitoring equipment being fitted to a driven pile in advance of dynamic pile testing (left). Statnamic pile testing equipment (right). Both images © Mike Brown

of specialist plant, but has the benefit of having a mass of only 5% of the equivalent kentledge and a limited surface footprint. Both dynamic and Statnamic pile testing should be assessed for vibration impact on adjacent structures similar to that required for driven piling. When positioning a test pile, its location in relation to the final construction piles should be considered. Where possible, test piles and reaction piles should be designed to form part of the final construction (working piles) reducing the need for additional piles. On very sensitive sites, this may affect the type of pile test chosen.

An alternative method of load testing piles is to use the bi-directional load cell method (eg Osterberg Cell). This system does not require additional reaction piles and so the impact on the archaeology will be reduced from only using the test pile itself. The bi-directional cell comprises a set of hydraulic jacks cast into the pile which then derives the reaction to the applied loading directly from the pile and ground both above and below the jacks, see www.loadtest.com for more information.

Pile testing is covered in detail by the *Handbook on Pile Load Testing,* produced by the Federation of Piling Specialists (2006).

Pile probing

It is not just pile installation that has the potential to cause damage to archaeological deposits. To investigate the presence of unknown below ground obstructions, pile probing is sometimes carried out on sites. This work does not necessarily take place during the piling contract, and can occur as part of the demolition or enabling works. Where this process does not fall into the construction phases, it can be difficult to manage, and it is best practice for it to be considered during the risk assessment process to ensure that its use is avoided on sites containing archaeological remains.

Probing for obstructions can be undertaken by several methods depending on the ground conditions, expected obstructions and their depth, as well as the proposed piling methodology. Common methods include: pushing a probe or rotating an auger into the ground at each pile location; or machine excavating a pit at pile locations. Probing is usually only undertaken to reach a depth of undisturbed natural ground, below which obstructions are not expected. Such methods and subsequent obstruction clearance though coring or excavations can significantly impact on archaeology.

The amount of probing can be mitigated in advance by undertaking a thorough desk study to overlay historical plans and the proposed pile layout and intrusive/non-intrusive investigations eg archaeological trenches and geophysical surveys.

Contaminated sites and piling

Many of the piling issues that concern archaeologists are similar to those that concern the Environment Agency regarding the effects of piling on groundwater. Pile installation on contaminated sites that overlie aquifers can give rise to increased leaching of pollutants to groundwater through vertical pathways created by the piling (Environment Agency 2001; Westcott *et al* 2003). On sites overlying fractured or fissured rock, or where there has previously been mineral working (ie deep mining), injection of grout (which might impact on shallow archaeological deposits) can also impact further down. At these sites, injection of grout could result in the migration of grout away from the bore over a very large area. Where possible, it is good practice for the archaeological and geotechnical investigations to be carried out alongside each other, to minimise the cost on developers with respect to site characterisation, risk assessment and risk management design. Further information on contamination assessment and management in relation to archaeological sites is given in Historic England guidance on Land Contamination and Archaeology.

5 Designing a sustainable foundation scheme

The NPPF requires developers to describe the significance of heritage assets, including that derived from their setting, affected by development. It is good practice to assess the archaeological and historical significance of a site at the earliest stage. This would include consulting the HER and assessing heritage assets using appropriate expertise. The archaeological potential of a proposed development site is set out in a desk-based assessment and explored further by field evaluation. This work can be in response to a development proposal where the impact of the scheme is already known, or to inform revisions or amendments to a design. In either case where the likely impacts of piling and foundation design are considered at the earliest stage, this allows relevant data to be collected, including foundation design of the existing and previous buildings on the site. This information will enable local planning authorities to consider the impact of the proposed scheme on the significance of heritage assets and to minimise harm. This helps to reduce risk and uncertainty in a development programme.

During the design process, the sharing of archaeological and engineering information will enable the development team to design a scheme to minimise harm to the character and significance of the archaeological remains. This will ensure that the most appropriate engineering and mitigation solutions are identified. It is therefore paramount that the character and significance of the archaeological deposits are drawn to the attention of the development team at an early stage so that the associated constraints can be considered as part of the design. Piling and building foundations can have a significant impact on archaeological remains. Piling may affect archaeological deposits over a wide area, for example by changing the site hydrogeology and it may be appropriate to consider the effects of the proposed works on deposits adjacent to the site.

The following sections of this chapter cover a series of different elements of the design process which will allow a sustainable foundation scheme to be developed. They focus on the avoidance or reduction of disturbance to archaeological remains and how that can be achieved, drawing on the technical explanations and principles outlined in the preceding chapters. Additional information is given in relation to human remains and waterlogged deposits which are particularly sensitive to the impacts of piling. By ensuring that all available alternative means of reducing archaeological impacts have been addressed in the formation of a foundation strategy, this document will assist in underpinning robust decision taking in this regard under the statutory planning system.

5.1 Pre-application discussion

Wherever possible it is recommended that developers seek early pre-application consultation with local planning authorities. Pre-application discussion is a key tool in managing risk for developers and can provide an early steer on the implications of development on a given site. It can give clarity on the likely scope and requirements of pre-determination archaeological work and associated evidence base requirements. It can also provide an understanding of any particular known risks or opportunities relating to archaeological remains within the site.

5.2 Collation of a robust evidence base

As part of the pre-application and pre-determination discussions, the earlier that supporting information is provided in the design process, the easier it will be to minimise harm and lower risk. Information to submit with a planning application (or pre-application discussion) might include:

- Desk based assessment (including assessment of significance)

    - Information about existing building foundations and basement levels

    - Deposit modelling

    - Tier 1 Hydrological Assessment (as appropriate, in accordance with guidance on **Preserving Archaeological Remains**)

- Field evaluation (if necessary, may include trial trenches, geophysical survey, geotechnical investigation, boreholes – some evaluation may include all of these techniques)

- An archaeological field evaluation report which sets out the findings of the evaluation, updates understanding of significance and the state of preservation of the archaeological remains, and assesses existing building impacts

All the information described above will provide valuable information to inform an approach for the foundation design to avoid or reduce archaeological impacts. It will also ensure that there is a clear understanding on which to devise an appropriate and proportionate scheme of archaeological mitigation where loss of such remains is considered to be justified.

5.3   Impact avoidance strategies

■ The most effective method for mitigating the impacts of piling on significant archaeological remains is to adopt an avoidance strategy, whereby piles are located away from archaeologically sensitive areas (Figure 31). In these cases foundations can be designed so that they impact only on the less sensitive areas or on areas of existing disturbance.

■ It is good practice for new foundations to be avoided in areas where there is potential for significant archaeological remains. Where this is not possible or feasible then a redesign of the foundations to include raft, ground beam, frame supports, or cantilevered structures above the significant archaeological horizon may be options.

■ Another option is to reduce the number of piles within groups by increasing the dimensions of the piles. Where the engineers have been closely involved with the mitigation process throughout, they will be able to design a piling layout that causes the least damage to archaeological remains and, where feasible, avoids the use of pile clusters.

Figure 31: Piles can be located to avoid structures identified in evaluation or a site strip. © MOLA

5.4 Pile re-use

Where a site has an existing piled foundation, it is good practice to consider their re-use and to carry out a feasibility study. An example of how a feasibility study could be agreed between a local authority and developer is outlined in case study 7.10. It is recommended that the feasibility study is carried out before demolition or enabling works, because these may damage the foundation.

The benefits of pile re-use are obvious since they reduce the need for new foundations, thus limiting impact on archaeological deposits. Frequently this is a technique that is being used in urban areas where, as the number of times a site is redeveloped increases, so does the number of service trenches, old foundations and other below-ground obstacles (Figure 32).

Over time, the area available for new foundations is dramatically reduced, and in some areas, for example London (where there are many other below ground obstructions), pile re-use may soon be the only feasible option. This problem is exacerbated by the fact that new buildings have a relatively short design-life (Butcher *et al* 2006a).

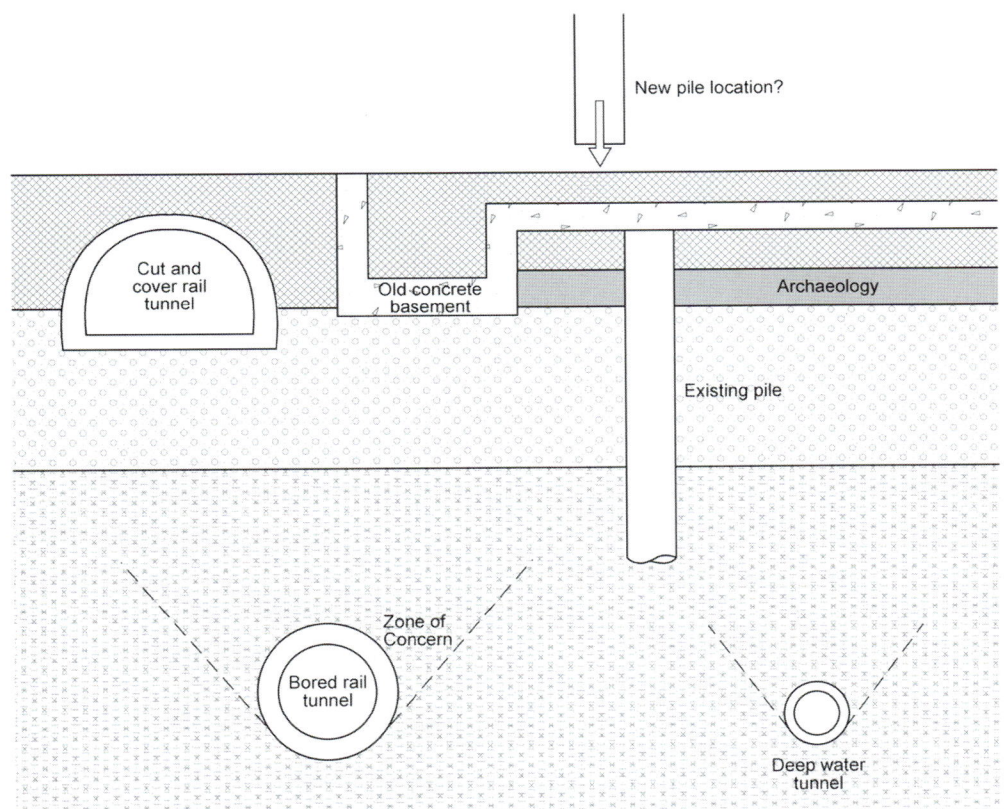

Figure 32: Ground congestion issues in urban centres severely restrict possible locations for new piles, making foundation re-use a very necessary technique. Image courtesy of the RuFUS Consortium 2006, and reproduced from Butcher *et al* 2006b

In some cases additional piles or foundations will be needed, or the existing piles may need to be strengthened, but even partial pile re-use will result in a reduction in the below-ground impact (Williams 2006). It is also possible to remove piles and re-use the locations for new piles if increased bearing capacity is needed (Hughes *et al* 2004, 101). This concentrates damage in areas that have already been affected by piling, although the process of removal is likely to be damaging and methodologies must be considered carefully.

Future pile re-use can be greatly assisted where Building Information Modelling (BIM) includes detailed information on the design and installation of piled foundations on the site.

Issues to consider

There are a large number of factors that need to be considered in any re-use strategy, including soil conditions, the structural capacity of the existing and new buildings, the character of the archaeological deposits across the site, and whether pile or pile location re-use is proposed.

A key factor in a successful pile-reuse strategy is a high-quality site investigation of the ground and existing foundation system, as set out in the CIRIA guide on foundation reuse (Chapman *et al* 2007).

Further issues include insurance and liability for old foundations, locating technical information about existing piles, testing the capacity of the old piles and the fact that the existing piles may be in the 'wrong' place for the new building. Many of these issues were evaluated by the EC funded project project **Reuse of Foundations for Urban Sites** (RuFUS), which published a handbook for foundation re-use (Butcher *et al* 2006a), and the proceedings of an international conference on the subject (Butcher *et al* 2006b).

One of the perceived drawbacks of foundation re-use is that each time a site is re-developed, economic pressures dictate that the new building will be larger than that being replaced, which usually means larger foundations. The possibility of over-engineering new piles for future re-use may develop, but this has cost implications which in the short term may be difficult to justify. However, by investing in piles with greater capacity in the present, substantial cost savings can then be passed on when the site is re-developed in the future. Additionally, it is possible that increased structural loads from larger buildings can be offset by using lighter building materials than were used in the original building.

Programme stage	Design stage	Construction stage	Building operation
Geological information	Design philosophy	As-built documents	As-built drawings
Geotechnical information	Design codes	Non-conformance reports	Maintenance records
Groundwater level	Design calculations	Construction documents	Environmental changes
Groundwater quality	Necessary bearing capacity	Programme of piling works	Inspections
Contaminated soil	Force combinations applied on each pile	Plant and equipment	Pile behaviour
Site conditions	Pile data	Test piling	Service life measurements
	Settlement limitations	Working documents	Structural alterations
	Protocol for foundation record	Site records	
		Pile installation records	
		Effects on nearby foundations and structures	
		Results from monitoring	

Table 3: Information relating to new piles that should be stored to enable future pile re-use (Butcher *et al* 2006a).

Collating data for future re-use

It is worth emphasising that new piles are significantly more likely to be re-used in the future if engineers have full information on the design and construction of these piles. Where archaeological deposits are particularly significant, consideration should also be given to instrumenting piles to be able to verify performance for future reuse. Recommendations for the type of information needed for future re-use are provided in the RuFUS handbook, summarised in Table 3.

5.5 Understanding piling impacts

Avoidance strategies are considered on a site-by-site basis, taking into account the scale and nature of the development and the archaeological potential. All piling operations will result in the physical destruction of archaeological deposits directly in the path of the pile and, while it is accepted that destruction will occur, there has been much discussion of what constitutes an acceptable level.

As is highlighted in Chapter 4, depending on the type of pile used, it is possible that disturbance to a zone larger than the size of the pile might occur. For example, recorded impacts from displacement piles are extremely variable, ranging from no perceptible change through to distinct zones of impact where the integrity of the stratigraphy equal to at least twice the width of the pile has been compromised.

When considering the likely level of impact from displacement piles, it is suggested that an area of impact equal to twice the width of the pile (ie one pile width either side of the pile centreline) is assumed, which equates to a fourfold increase in the area of pile impact; it is this value that must be factored in when assessing the harm to the significance of archaeological remains on site. Furthermore, where three or more piles are placed within a cluster, the area within this cluster will be very hard to interpret in the future. For the purposes of assessing harm to the significance of archaeological remains on site, the impact to this area is usually be considered to be high.

Local authority planning and archaeological officers need to be aware of the cumulative impact of re-development on a site, which makes later interpretation more difficult. In these cases, foundation re-use, both of the existing foundations or their locations, may be a beneficial mitigation method. In other cases, archaeological excavation may represent a more appropriate option than any further attempts to preserve the site within the development.

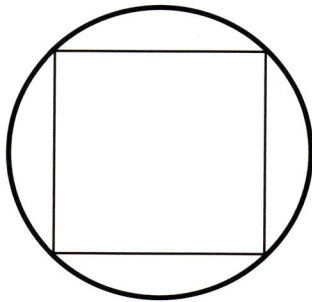

Figure 33: Recommended diameter for pre-augering (circle) shown along with the square pile, with the same distance across the diagonal as the diameter of the auger hole.

5.6 Pre-augering displacement pile locations

One method to reduce potential physical damage to sediments adjacent to preformed displacement piles is to pre-auger the pile locations. This technique was trialled on two sites which were subsequently excavated archaeologically (Davies 2003; Rayner 2005). In both cases the excavation demonstrated that the impact of the subsequent displacement piling was limited to the area already disturbed by the pre-augering.

In order that this technique is successful, it is recommended that the auger diameter is equal to the diagonal of the pile and augered to below the depth of known archaeological deposits (Figure 33). The material disturbed in pre-augering should remain in place by rotating the auger in the opposite direction to penetration during withdrawal.

5.7 Obstructions to piling

When piles are to be installed on sites where previous foundations or substantial structural archaeological remains are suspected (stone walls/foundations, etc), then the piling contractor should be made aware of this issue; the applicant should have already identified the potential for obstructions within the risk assessment process.

Where non-displacement piles are used, it is possible that tools capable of cutting directly through these obstructions could be used. In these instances it is essential that the piling contractor is aware of these issues at the time that the work is specified, so that the right equipment and a methodology capable of overcoming such obstructions can be identified.

Where it is not possible to cut directly through obstructions, or preformed driven piling is undertaken, two options are available: either remove the obstructions through excavation from the surface or relocate the pile(s). Where archaeological remains are present, localised archaeological excavation of the remains forming the obstruction is likely to be needed, which could delay the piling programme. This is why it is important that a full understanding of the location, significance and state of preservation of archaeological remains present on site is compiled before this work takes place.

Locating obstructions is potentially a very damaging stage of construction as, quite reasonably, developers seek to avoid unexpected ground conditions. This work may not be part of the main piling programme, but included within a separate demolition or enabling contract. A methodology detailing steps to be taken when encountering obstructions should be prepared for each site and in some cases it may be appropriate for an archaeologist to be present during demolition or enabling works to ensure the methodology agreed by all parties to address this issue, is adhered to on site. In cases where a total site strip to the top of archaeological remains is undertaken as part of the evaluation and mitigation process, obstructions can be more readily identified, enabling a suitable methodology for removal (if necessary) to be agreed.

Removing obstructions that cannot be directly bored through may involve probing or pre-augering with diamond or chisel cutting tips. However, contractors must not engage in uncontrolled machine clearance of obstructions as this can result in a collateral loss of archaeological integrity as the area around an obstruction is checked thoroughly for obstructions.

5.8   Piling and waterlogged deposits

Understanding the full impacts of piling on waterlogged deposits is complex, and requires a thorough knowledge of the site hydrogeology. Appendix 3 of the guidance on Preserving Archaeological Remains provides detailed information on undertaking a water environment assessment.

Cofferdams constructed from augered secant or driven sheet piles, whether used to control water ingress during construction or in flood defence barriers, may impact on waterlogged archaeological remains by altering water levels. A water environment study, conducted to inform the decision-taking process, would provide an assessment of groundwater flow and availability and can be used to consider the effects of any barriers on water (or soil moisture) levels on site. Where the barriers are long-term there is every possibility that waterlogged deposits may be cut off from hydraulic recharge and decay as a result, rendering long-term preservation unviable.

The chemical impact of pile concrete from non-displacement piles on waterlogged deposits is not yet fully understood, and although two field tests (Williams *et al* 2008) did not identify any significant impacts, there still remains the potential that some chemical damage may occur. During the time that the pile cures, there is a potential risk that the migration of chemicals from the pile grout/concrete may locally affect the groundwater. The impact of this will, to a large degree, depend upon the nature of the waterlogged deposits, and the rate of groundwater flow. Deposits with a high hydraulic conductivity, such as gravel, may have fairly rapid groundwater movement, but organic-rich, peat-like deposits typically have a low hydraulic conductivity, meaning groundwater movement will be limited and therefore the potential risk is significantly reduced. This could be further reduced by the adoption of preformed piling solutions or, when casting of concrete in the ground cannot be avoided, the installation of a permanent casing. Evidence from the excavation of previous non-displacement piles in similar soil and groundwater conditions would help to refine the risks outlined above.

Concerns exist regarding the possibility of piles puncturing impermeable layers that contribute to the preservation of waterlogged deposits, particularly in urban environments where there are known to be perched water tables. Mitigation for development, where waterlogging is known to occur above the natural groundwater level, should include an appraisal of the proposed foundation design and consideration of a solution which avoids impacts. Model-scale research (Hird *et al* 2006) indicates that the most important factor is the thickness of the aquitard (the impermeable layer restricting groundwater flow). Where piling is the only option on waterlogged sites with perched water tables, then the use of permanent rather than temporary casings on non-displacement piles should be considered, as the removal of temporary casings may also disrupt the aquitard. Further information can be found in publications such as the Environment Agency's Decommissioning Redundant Boreholes and Wells and the Scottish Environment Protection Agency's Good Practice for Decommissioning Redundant Boreholes and Wells.

5.9   Piling and burial grounds

Burial grounds contain human skeletal remains and associated items such as monuments, coffins and grave goods. They constitute some of our most significant archaeological sites, containing important sources of information about our past. In addition, they may also contain structural remains such as paths, vaults and earlier phases of church buildings which enable us to understand the development and use of the site in tandem with what we can learn from the skeletal population.

When dealing with burial grounds of any denomination, their excavation, study and archiving require consideration of sensitive ethical and legal considerations (see APABE, 2017). For this reason the avoidance of disturbance is the preferred option, but any disturbance must be clearly and convincingly justified. The significance of all the archaeology, which includes the skeletal remains, should be understood prior to designing foundations for new schemes. The Ministry of Justice, who would need to provide a licence to undertake disturbance to a burial ground, (other than those of the Church of England in active use, which are subject to Faculty Jurisdiction) would not normally permit piling in such locations and this principle is upheld here.

An alternative to piling is the use of ground beams and raft foundations. This approach to foundation design presents a viable alternative to piling where human remains will be impacted and has been successful in many development situations (see for example case study provided by Shilston and Fletcher 1998). However, its use does not necessarily avoid all impacts and will require archaeological excavation within the area where human remains will be disturbed, ie the area of ground beams. Where such a foundation design can be employed, certainty is required that the human remains can be safely preserved below the raft construction. Although more burials may be impacted upon than through piling, this approach does not lead to destruction without record of both burials and other unknown archaeology (for example, see Figure 22).

Piling should only be considered if wholly exceptional circumstances prevail, and the public benefit outweighs the harm caused to the significance of the archaeological remains. In such circumstances a detailed project plan should be put into place, covering evaluation, excavation, foundation design, movement of piling rigs and exclusion zones (for instance over vaults). Archaeological excavation should take place within the area of the pile caps as a minimum, to ensure that no human remains are piled through. Ideally, the excavation should lead to the recovery of complete rather than partial skeletons, so that an archaeologically coherent and meaningful analysis can take place.

5.10 Reporting

It is imperative to the success of future foundation re-use schemes that all available design and construction data for current foundations are stored in a suitable location such as the site archive or local Historic Environment Record. Data should include the final pile locations, loading capacity, test results, and as-built drawings. Other information such as the engineers' design report, contractors' method statements and more detailed designs should form part of the site archive.

Where excavation has provided information on the impact of previous foundations on archaeological remains, these impacts should be recorded as part of the reporting process, as they provide an indication of the impacts of similar foundations solutions planned for the site (or surrounding areas).

5.11 Summary

This edition of guidance does not prescribe the percentage of piling that might be appropriate on any given development, as on different sites, the archaeological deposits and the significance of the site will have a bearing on what is appropriate. The understanding of these issues will depend on the quality and quantity of information available from the site evaluation and understanding of previous truncation.

The guidance also does not contain specific advice on the amount of and methods of evaluation. In some places, a total site strip to the top of archaeological deposits with selective further sampling of deeper deposits has been identified as the most effective method of site characterisation; this method also provides information to aid in the micro-siting of foundations to avoid harm to areas of significance. In other locations, different methods may suit site constraints and the nature of the archaeological remains. Local planning authority archaeologists are in the best position to make these judgements on a case by case basis.

On many archaeological sites developed in the last 30 years, developers and their project teams have routinely designed foundation schemes where new piling impacts have been kept to a very low percentage of the overall site area. Reducing foundation impacts on archaeological remains is thus technically feasible. Equally, unless there are specific reasons for over-engineering a foundation scheme (for example to allow for future foundation re-use), it is an unnecessary expense to use more piles than is necessary to meet the design requirements and technical standards.

The key issues that need to be considered to avoid or reduce harm from piling on any site containing archaeological remains are:

■ Evaluation and site investigation results

■ Location, depth, character, significance and state of preservation of archaeological remains

■ The impact of previous development on this site on the significance and state of preservation of archaeological remains

■ The combined impact of the existing, proposed and previous development on the significance and state of preservation of archaeological remains

Early and constant discussion of these issues with the local authority archaeological advisers, and the use of the risk assessment methodology outlined in section 5 will help all sides come to an understanding about what represents a sustainable foundation solution for a given site.

Issues to consider when designing a sustainable foundation solution are presented in Table 4.

Pile Type	Mitigation
All pile types	Adopt 'avoidance strategy' and avoid use of piles in areas of archaeological sensitivity where possible. Where piling is unavoidable, limit extent of physical destruction as far as possible to avoid harm to significance. The impact of all ground intrusions, including ground beams and pile caps needs to be considered. Burial grounds should not be piled. Need to take into account potential pre-construction impacts, such as pile probing, on-site effects from piling equipment (plant), and associated infrastructure, such as piling mats, concrete plants etc
Large displacement piles	Zone of impact is potentially greater than diameter of pile, therefore calculate percentage loss of area in building footprint using four times the pile area, unless there is evidence of the impact of past piling activity recovered through excavation.
Small displacement piles	Sheet – If waterlogged remains are present, assess potential impacts on groundwater flow and recharge of deposits through undertaking water environment study to understand long-term effects on water-table and water chemistry. H-section – Not recommended for waterlogged deposits due to possible migration and oxygen ingress.
Non-displacement piles	Consider use of suitable cutting tools where obstructions are likely to be encountered. For secant walls see above for sheet piles. CFA – Avoid on sites where modern and archaeological structural remains likely unless suitable cutting heads can be used to cut through obstructions, or where site strip has allowed these to be identified in full.
Vibro ground improvement techniques	Require further investigation, but are likely to be extremely damaging to archaeology and should be avoided where possible.

Table 4: Key foundation issues to consider.

6 Risk assessment

As information about the significance of a site is obtained, through assessment and evaluation, it is good practice to consider and assess the risks of potential impacts.

Risk assessment forms a conventional tool used by project teams to identify, evaluate, avoid or control risk. This section lays out an approach to assessing risk to the significance of archaeological deposits within development. We recommend this is begun at pre-planning stages and continuously updated during design development, forming part of the documentation submitted in support of applications for planning permission.

6.1 Objective

To propose a robust, effective and transparent decision making process that allows project team to select appropriate foundation methods and control measures when working on archaeological sites.

Design and avoidance measures

In many cases it will be possible to remove a potentially adverse impact on the significance of the archaeological deposits by the design and specification of avoidance measures. These could be based, for example, on changes to the building location/structural arrangement, foundation option or changes to the piling installation method.

6.2 Risk assessment method

The recommended risk assessment process to be carried out by the project team is given in Table 5. It provides a framework for the project team to carry out (with the input of appropriate archaeological advice) a risk assessment to select the most appropriate foundation option and to justify this choice with appropriate design and avoidance measures. It is good practice for this process to start at the pre-planning stage concurrent with design development. It works best as a continuous iterative process with design and avoidance measures updated as new information becomes available from desk based research and site investigations.

Below is guide to the column heading and the type of information to be entered:

Foundation options

There could be various different alternatives to provide a sound foundation to a building. For example this could be a raft, slab and ground beams, groups of small diameter piles, or a reduced number of large diameter piles. All feasible foundation designs should be considered, using Table 5. For the various piling methods see Section 3.

Impacts

Six key impacts have been identified and these remain constant for each foundation option. The six impacts are:

- Enabling and temporary works (operations to prepare the site for construction)

- Installation damage (including vibration)

- Hydrogeology / compression / chemical / contamination

- Ground substructure (clusters, pile caps etc.)

- Cumulative attrition

- Post-construction remedial and maintenance activities

Hazards

The hazards represent the threat to the archaeological deposits from each impact dependent on the foundation option. These can include physical damage, changes to ground conditions (hydrology, contamination, chemistry), and simply through the cumulative impact of further new development. These threats should be clearly assessed in this column.

Design / avoidance measures

This column should be informed by the available information and continuously updated throughout design development as new information becomes available from desk based research and site investigations.

This column should suggest solutions to protect the significance of the archaeological deposits.

Uncertainties

Use this column for any additional risk. It should identify areas that are not yet defined.

Foundation options	Impact	Hazards	Design / avoidance measures	Uncertainties
	Enabling and temporary works (operations to prepare the site for construction), including obstructions			
	Installation damage (including vibration)			
	Hydrogeology / compression / chemical / contamination			
	Ground substructure (clusters, pile caps etc.)			
	Cumulative attrition			
	Post-construction remedial and maintenance activities			

Table 5. Blank risk assessment form.

7 Case studies

7.1 Pile pre-augering: JunXion, Lincoln

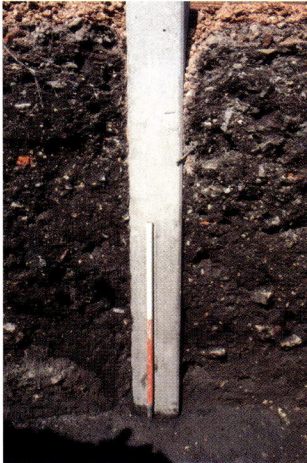

An opportunity arose to test the potential for pre-augering concrete driven pile locations to reduce the drag down adjacent deposits, at a site in Lincoln. The piling contractor wanted to demonstrate that the area of impact from driven piles could be better controlled if the locations were pre-augered to below the depth of the archaeological deposits. They particularly wanted to use this technique along one side of the site to reduce piling vibration on the printing presses of the local newspaper, housed next door.

The methodology entailed pre-augering the pile location with a 350mm diameter auger to a depth of 3-4m which was then withdrawn whilst rotating in the opposite direction. This left the soil in the ground, but disrupted it sufficiently to make the insertion of 250mm square piles easier. The auger size was chosen to match closely the distance across the pile diagonal (353mm). As the technique had not apparently been used before on an archaeological site, it was agreed that an evaluation of its impact on archaeological remains would be carried out.

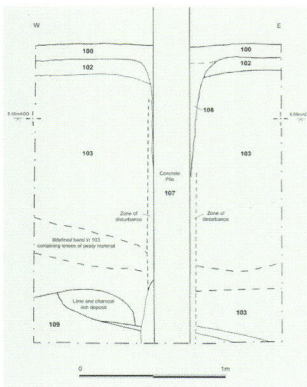

Following excavation, no evidence of disturbance outside the area of the auger (ie 350mm) could be identified (see Figures 34 & 35). Since the potential damage estimated for the driven piles on this site was twice the width of the pile (c 500mm), this therefore represented a reduction in the potential area of damage that might have occurred from driven piling alone. In this case, evidence from an example pile, driven without first pre-augering, indicated that down-dragging of material and its impact on these particular deposits was also limited to a zone no greater than that of the auger (ie 350mm). On this basis, for this particular site, it was decided that there was no need to pre-auger the majority of pile locations on the site (except those adjacent to the printing press).

Figures 34 and 35: Piling mat carried down adjacent to the pile, the JunXion, Lincoln (top) © ARCUS. Section drawing of sediment deformation from the JunXion, Lincoln (bottom). Image from Davies 2003.

7.2 Steel screw piles: Salisbury

This technique was used on a sensitive archaeological site in Salisbury (Figure 36). The piles were made up of a number of curved spirals of steel of varying diameters connected to a central shaft (as shown in Figure 23). Piles, which had a 250kN capacity (T Sheward pers comm), were screwed into the ground to depths of 5m (Sheward 2003). Benefits were that it was unnecessary to remove spoil associated with any piling operation, or to bring piling materials to the site through the city's narrow streets. Additionally, the piles can be removed by unscrewing at a later date theoretically causing very limited damage to below-ground deposits.

Figure 36: Screw piles being installed. © Tim Sheward

7.3 Pile re-use: Ramada Encore Hotel, Mickelgate, York

Figure 37: Exterior of the hotel which is built largely on re-used piles.

The previous building on the site was the offices of the Yorkshire Co-operative Society, constructed in the 1960s. The site was acquired by a developer to build a hotel. During discussions with the City Archaeologist, the developer was informed of the likely archaeological potential of the site, which was situated within the medieval town walls, not far from the riverside, and therefore likely to contain well preserved organic material. On the basis of that discussion, the developer produced a plan to re-use the foundations of the existing building, thereby reducing the potential need for, and cost of archaeological evaluation (Figures 37 and 38). The scheme, which included the re-use of all 110 previous piles, needed a further 17 installed in three discrete locations. This meant that over most of the rest of the site, no ground disturbance occurred. Any below ground impact was further mitigated because the building was constructed on the existing ground slab with archaeological recording during the installation of services and pile caps, none of which were deep enough to encounter significant archaeological deposits.

This scheme was very successful, mainly because the potential for re-use had been highlighted early enough in the design phase of the scheme, and was led by the developer, who was keen to reduce the risk to the scheme of having to deal with archaeological material (Williams and Butcher 2006).

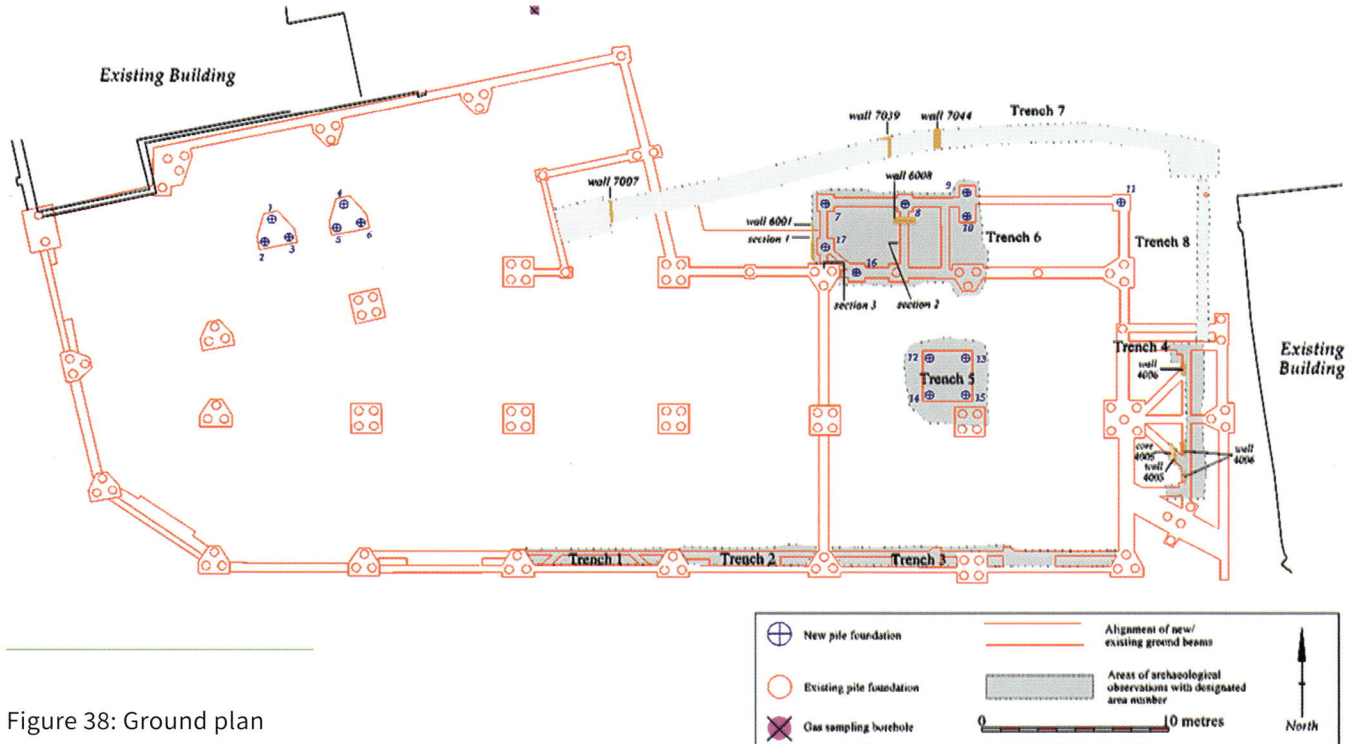

Figure 38: Ground plan showing location of previous and new piles. © York Archaeological Trust

7.4 Pile avoidance and redesign: 43 The Highway, Shadwell, London

An exceptionally well-preserved Roman building was discovered during excavation in advance of development (Figure 39). Roman remains had been anticipated following evaluation, but not the quality of the building and extent of its survival. It was considered by the archaeological curator to be a find of national significance and therefore preservation of the building was recommended and agreed by all parties. However, planning permission subject to a condition to archaeologically record and excavate the site had been granted for a multi-storey residential block of apartments.

The site is located in the Thames floodplain, on inherently unstable alluvial sediments, requiring substantial piled foundations through river silts and gravels. Discussions took place on exactly which aspects of the Roman archaeology needed to be preserved and what, if anything, could be preserved by record. It was decided that all intact structural elements needed to be preserved while some spaces between walls could be fully excavated, recorded, backfilled and then piled through. The use of detailed digital plans of the archaeology was extremely important to compare with the proposed foundation plan including pile locations. The foundations were redesigned to allow development while retaining the building intact. The proposed CFA technique was retained and no pile dimensions had to be changed. Piles were relocated to areas between the Roman walls and hypocaust *pilae*, with as much clearance as possible between pile locations and the Roman building. The building was backfilled to an agreed specification involving geotextile, inert sand, and then graded spoil from the site. CFA piles were then carefully located and installed, securing the safety of the building.

Figure 39: The Shadwell bathhouse. © Pre-Construct Archaeology Ltd

7.5 Communication and design changes: The Curtain Theatre, Shoreditch

When proposals were initially scoped to develop the area thought to incorporate the location of the Curtain Theatre, one of the earliest Shakespearean playhouses in London, the developer was enthusiastic about incorporating the remains into the new mixed use scheme as a public display. Archaeological evaluation was undertaken in difficult circumstances as the site was heavily built up, but traces were found of a Tudor polygonal building, tentatively identified as the playhouse. The design for the new scheme progressed, designing foundations carefully around a roughly circular space, to enable the playhouse to be preserved when finally revealed.

After demolition began on the site, further excavation led to an exciting, but unexpected discovery. The playhouse was well preserved but rectangular, rather than polygonal. By this time plans were advanced and required a significant redesign to incorporate a square playhouse into a round hole. The new buildings, including a substantial tower, would be hard up against and slightly over-sailing the playhouse, and require basements as well as a substantial piling scheme.

The developer was extremely supportive of protecting the archaeology (the site is nationally important) and the design and engineering teams worked with archaeologists to examine every pile location where there was a possible conflict and make adjustments to avoid the most significant elements of the site. Substantial concrete slabs were present in the ground, which form one element of the foundation design but no piles were suitable for re-use, owing to the much larger scale of the new build.

Several plunge piles were carefully inserted in the archaeological area between the masonry, in areas crucial for the new tower. These plunge piles allowed the construction of the superstructure to begin before the basement had been formed, helping with the programme.

In addition to the permanent piling scheme, a temporary secant pile wall was built around the playhouse, to effectively box it in to protect the remains during construction of the new scheme. The partial reduction of this secant wall allows the public presentation of the remains. The success of this scheme, and the way in which new information was incorporated into redesigns has been possible because there was early evaluation which highlighted the significance of the site and constant communication between archaeologists, engineers and designers to accommodate the complex archaeological remains present on site.

7.6 Prior information used to reduce harm: Bloomberg European Headquarters, City of London

Archaeological evaluation in advance of the construction of Bloomberg's European Headquarters revealed that fragmentary remains of the eastern third of the Roman Temple of Mithras survived on the site, together with an antechamber or narthex just beyond the proposed new building boundary. The temple was discovered first in the 1950s and mostly relocated to a new site 100m away from its original location. As part of the Bloomberg development, a new reconstruction was to be built as close as possible to the original site. It was not possible to put the newly discovered remains on display due to their vulnerable condition and the waterlogged ground conditions. The decision was therefore taken to preserve them beneath the existing basement slab and to build the new reconstruction at the original Roman ground level but a small distance to the west of the surviving remains (see Figure 40).

To accomplish this, a large transfer beam was needed to carry the loads of a structural perimeter column that would have otherwise required a foundation pile to be located through the narthex. Another pile position was moved 500mm to avoid masonry remains of the narthex and was constructed within a permanent steel casing. This was to prevent disturbance of the ground close to the pile by the complete removal of the pile casings. The transfer beam was also designed to be at least 500mm above the highest surviving archaeological remains. These adjustments were possible because of the detail provided by the archaeological investigations on site, and constant dialogue between all parties.

Figure 40: Finalising the reconstruction of the Temple of Mithras. © MOLA

7.7 Ground-truthing a lower impact solution: Bloomberg European Headquarters, City of London

The north-east corner of the site was allocated for a new London Underground station entrance for Bank Station – requiring deep excavation to meet the level of the Waterloo and City Line. This was also the area of the site with the deepest archaeological deposits extending to up to 12m below modern ground level. The design for the new station entrance was not finalised by the time the site became available for archaeological excavation. In particular the line of the perimeter of the station box was not fixed and this meant that secant pile wall could not be installed. As the archaeology was such a big component of the project and on the critical path, the project team wanted to get started as soon as possible. An alternative perimeter retention solution was needed to support the surrounding streets and to facilitate safe working conditions for the archaeologists.

The solution was to use 15m driven steel sheet piles instead of the secant wall, which could be removed if required (see Figures 41 and 42). In order to avoid destructive pile probing for the sheets, geoarchaeologists augered the line of the piles at 1m intervals, gaining valuable samples and information (Figure 43). Because of the great depth of the archaeology in this area, the use of sheet piles instead of a pile wall meant that a large volume of approximately 350m³ of archaeology of very high significance (including Roman timber property boundaries and wooden writing tablets) was not impacted by the construction of a pile wall (see Figure 44).

Figures 41, 42, 43 and 44: Engineers sketch of the shoring solution (above top) © McGees. Excavation underway using sheet piles for retention. The engineers were able to use these sheets for the final structure (above middle). Geoarchaeologists augering to check for obstructions and also evaluate deep deposits (above). The type of Roman deposits that would have otherwise been destroyed by secant pile wall (which would have extended out by approx. 1m from line of sheets) (right). All other images © MOLA

7.8 Prior information and close cooperation: Cannon Place, City of London

Cannon Place was a very complex commercial office development involving the construction of new piled foundations adjacent to and beneath a live railway station. The position of columns and supporting piles was limited by platforms and existing 19th century brick viaducts. The project also involved the re-use of 1970s foundations. Cannon Place is located over the Governor's Palace Scheduled Monument.

Figure 45: Roman masonry of the Governor's Palace, showing the complex working environment. © MOLA

The archaeological project involved several phases of evaluation to understand the potential impacts on nationally important Roman remains and extensive discussions between the project team, particularly the engineers, archaeologists and planners to achieve a piling design that minimised the damage to archaeological deposits.

It is easiest to focus on one pile location to illustrate the approach taken. Pile Group 9 was located partly within the area occupied by the 19th century brick viaduct and also in an area where the evaluation had revealed a substantial Roman masonry wall associated with the Governor's Palace complex (Figure 45). The project engineers designed a mini-pile solution. This allowed mini-pile groups and pile caps to be formed to fit closely around the masonry, with Terram, Flexcell Board and Visqueen providing protection between the pile structures and archaeology. The mini-pile clusters behave like a much larger pile, structurally.

The sequence of archaeological work for Pile Group 9 was as follows: the maximum area of impact 2.5m x 2m was marked out accurately on the slab and the concrete broken out by contractors. Modern material was removed to the top of archaeological deposits under archaeological supervision. Shoring was installed by contractors. Archaeological hand excavation and recording of all 'soft' deposits within the area of the trench was carried out down to base of archaeological deposits. Provision had been made for the trimming of any Roman masonry to ensure piling would not be obstructed. In the event this was not needed for this pile group. Protective materials were put in place and metal sleeves were installed in the mini pile locations and secured in position. The excavation area was backfilled with bentonite cement to ensure that the sleeves were held in place during piling. The brick viaduct arch was trimmed to allow the mini-piling rig to access the area required and piling operations took place. The pile cap area was subsequently excavated and new pile cap constructed.

7.9 Evaluation informed pile locations: Former All Saints Brewery, Leicester

This site, located within the walls of Roman and medieval Leicester, was proposed for redevelopment involving the construction of a ten-storey apartment block with wings ranged around a central courtyard. It was formerly occupied by a 1960s office block and a late 19th century brewery. Following demolition of existing buildings, a programme of archaeological trial trenching was undertaken in 2012 and 2014, revealing evidence for a Roman street, structures of the 2nd-4th C, part of the medieval street frontage and fragments of a medieval hospital (see Figure 46). The results suggested that, of the footprint of the proposed building, about 15% occupied areas of low archaeological significance with extensive truncation from cellars; 24% contained material of moderate significance with the survival of some stratification and 61% of the area was of high significance, with extensive archaeological remains and little previous disturbance.

Figure 46: Evaluation trenches showing the survival of a range of Roman archaeological remains. © University of Leicester Archaeological Services (ULAS)

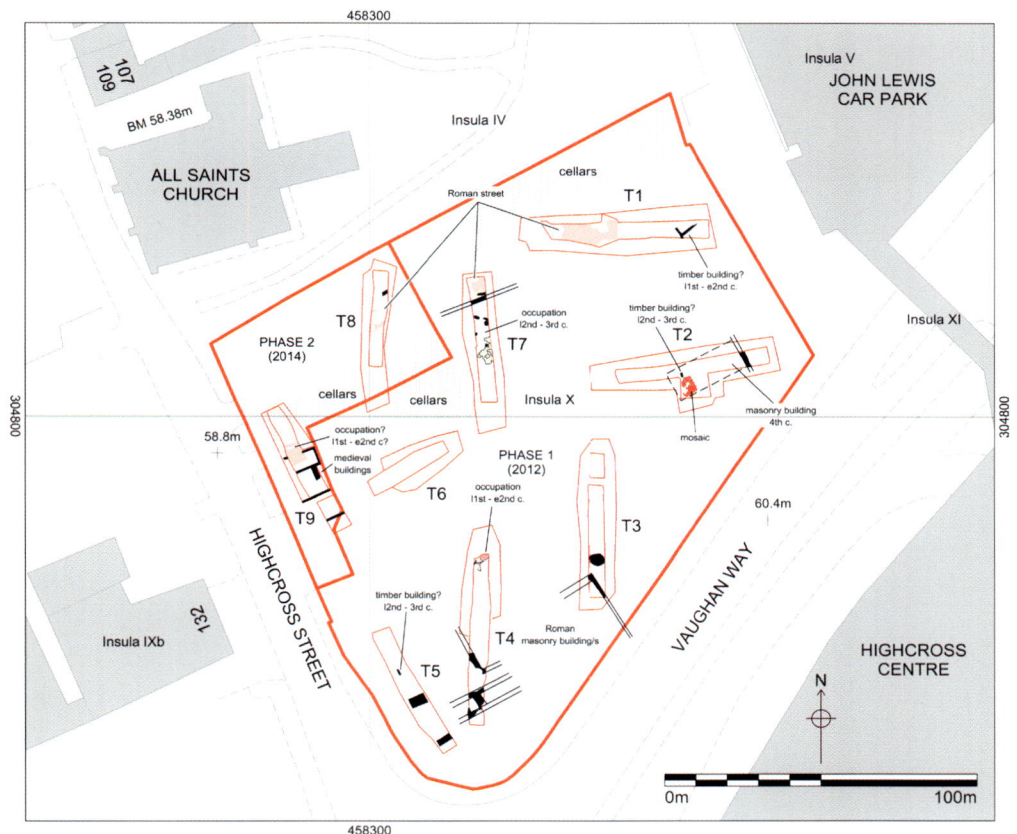

CFA piling was proposed for the new building. To come up with a sustainable foundation solution, archaeologists worked closely with the engineers to achieve a design solution which would minimise the archaeological impact. One result of these discussions was that pile caps would be accommodated within the 2m depth of late medieval garden soils and modern overburden which existed across the site. This meant that harm to archaeological remains would mostly be from the piles themselves.

The pile grid would disturb about 3% of the proposed footprint. To ensure that piling did not harm the significance of the site, (derived from complex structural remains, including fragments of a mosaic – see Figure 47), the footprint of the proposed building was stripped under archaeological supervision to the top of the archaeology. The deposits, thus exposed, were then cleaned, recorded and sampled to assess date and significance. This allowed the specific impact of individual piles to be assessed. Where harm to significance was deemed unacceptable, adjustments were made to pile positions and in some areas, the potential loss of significance was managed by excavating the area in advance of piling.

Figure 47: A section of Roman mosaic under excavation. © University of Leicester Archaeological Services (ULAS)

The results of this assessment indicated that for the most part, the piles would pass through deposits whose significance would not be harmed by the piling (as they would remain intelligible in the future). No further archaeological investigation was required in those areas. Elsewhere, some of the pile positions were re-adjusted (by moving them or spreading out pile clusters) to avoid specific structural remains and/or areas of existing 1960s piling where further development would render the archaeology uninterpretable.

This left three areas where the piles would go through complex archaeology, including walls, a hypocaust, a mosaic and associated deposits. Given that the CFA piles would cause unacceptable harm to significance in these areas (and in some cases, would not be capable of passing through archaeological obstructions without them being cleared first), the decision was taken to undertake a programme of limited excavation to address these impacts. Rather than targeting individual piles for excavation which would potentially provide meaningless results, larger areas were selected based on groups of piles.

The overall result of this foundation strategy has been an archaeological plan of the whole footprint of the proposed building at the level of the uppermost archaeological deposits; a sample of such deposits to clarify their, nature, extent, date and significance (as with an evaluation) and the full archaeological excavation of a small number of areas where the harm to significance would have been greatest. This included the lifting of the mosaic pavement which would be affected by a pile. This foundation strategy was made possible by good prior information, from adjacent sites and previous phases of evaluation, as well as regular communication and a developer willing to work collaboratively to find the most appropriate solution that ensured that harm to significance from piling was kept to a minimum. Figure 48 shows a summary of the information gathered from prior work (for example the Roman road grids shown in yellow), the evaluation and excavation, indicating the areas in blue where targeted full excavation took place.

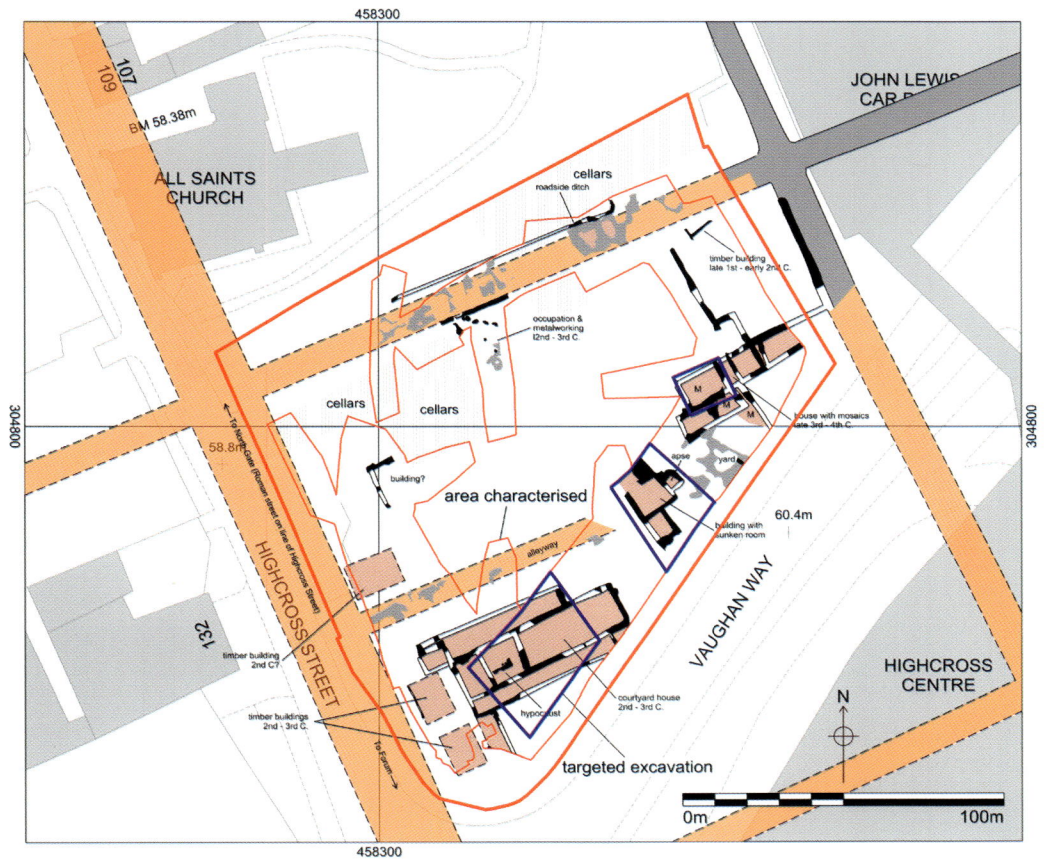

Figure 48: Summary plan of the site. The thick red line is the extent of the site, the thinner line the area of site strip and excavation. © University of Leicester Archaeological Services (ULAS)

7.10 Pile reuse planning conditions agreed in advance with developer, former Gloucester Prison site

On sites with significant archaeological remains or potential, it is good practice for the developer to seek an agreed approach with the local authority prior to the submission of the application. Early discussion on mitigation requirements and approaches can usefully be followed by consultation on the wording and structure of draft conditions. A developer who feels that they have had an input into the process and whose concerns are understood is more likely to take a positive and co-operative approach going forward.

In the case of pile-reuse, the pre-application process is a good time to highlight the benefits that pile reuse can bring in terms of cost and risk management. Conditions can be agreed that allow for the undertaking of feasibility studies for pile reuse if such work cannot be undertaken prior to determination. Whilst it may not be reasonable to require pile reuse, it is possible to require that a feasibility study is undertaken and separately, to require approval of the proposed foundation design.

This was the approach taken at the Former Prison site in Gloucester where archaeological evaluation had shown that fragments of a 12th and 13th century castle survived beneath the site (shown in Figure 49). It should be emphasised that these conditions were agreed in advance with the developer and only relate to part of the site. They were designed to work as two conditions undertaken consecutively. The first condition required a feasibility study be undertaken (in this case for just part of the site – but it could apply to the whole site). The second required approval by the local planning authority of the final foundation design. This final foundation design would be informed by the results of the feasibility study. If foundation reuse was possible this would have clear benefits to the developer as it would reduce the requirement for other forms of archaeological mitigation.

Figure 49: The castle keep found during evaluation. © Cotswold Archaeology

The planning conditions used in this case study were written in 2017 before the revision of the NPPF in 2018; the updated paragraph numbers should be used in any new conditions produced from this point forward.

Condition: Feasibility Study for Pile Reuse

'No development or demolition shall commence until a methodology for the undertaking of a feasibility study for the reuse of existing piled foundations in the area of block H (as referenced on plan 1803/004 amendment P1) has been submitted to and approved by the local planning authority in writing. This shall include provision for pre- and post-demolition analysis. Subsequently no construction of Block H shall commence until the feasibility study has been submitted to and approved in writing by the Local Planning Authority.'

Reason: To minimise impact to heritage assets of high significance by establishing the prospect for re-use of existing piled foundation or alternatively locating piles in areas of existing disturbance, in accordance with paragraphs 131, 132 and 139 of the NPPF and Policy SD8 of the Gloucester, Cheltenham and Tewkesbury Joint Core Strategy Adopted 2017.

This condition is intended to enable the undertaking of a feasibility study into the reuse of existing piled foundations in the area of block H. This is intended to be a physical assessment of the piles undertaken by an appropriately qualified structural engineer (prior to and following demolition to slab). At the end of the process a report will need to be produced outlining if reuse is viable and what potential options are available. This report will inform the City Council's consideration of the proposed foundation design when submitted.

Condition: details of foundations, groundworks and services

'No works below existing ground level shall commence until a detailed scheme showing the complete scope and arrangement of the foundation design and ground works of the proposed development (including pile type and methodology, drains and services, and for Block H shall take into consideration the results of the Feasibility Study approved under Condition X – above) has been submitted to and approved in writing by the Local Planning Authority. Development shall only take place in accordance with the approved scheme.'

Reason: The site may contain significant heritage assets. The Council requires that disturbance or damage by foundations and related works is minimised, and that archaeological remains are, where appropriate, preserved *in situ*. This accords with paragraphs 131, 132 and 139 of the NPPF and Policy SD8 of the Gloucester, Cheltenham and Tewkesbury Joint Core Strategy Adopted 2017.

It is important to note that the scope and arrangement of the foundation design can only be finalised once the feasibility study on pile reuse in block H has been undertaken. The Archaeological mpact and Mitigation statement will need to be updated accordingly.

8 Supporting information – pile impacts

This chapter provides further detail to statements made in Chapter 4. It contains information from field-scale observations of piling impacts recorded adjacent to previous foundations as well as data from model-scale research.

8.1 Driven preformed piles: physical impacts

Physical impacts of driven preformed piles on archaeological remains have been recognised in a number of studies (Biddle 1994; Dalwood *et al* 1994). Such displacement is demonstrated in the image from Farrier Street, Worcester (Dalwood *et al* 1994), which shows down-dragging of deposits resulting from pile installation (Figure 50). Dalwood *et al* suggest (on the basis of calculations made from excavations adjacent to piles in Worcester), that the area of the site affected by piling operations was up to six times larger than originally predicted. Although numerous anecdotes of pile damage exist, few comprehensive studies have been published. A survey of 46 Historic Environment Records for reports of piling impacts produced only three examples (from 17 replies) where piling impacts had been recorded (Davies 2004). At the Marefair, Northampton, significant distortion was recorded adjacent to one of the piles (480mm in diameter), with disturbance up to 250mm either side. The total area of damage had a radius of approximately 1.0m and vertical displacement of over 1.0m, (Northamptonshire Archaeology undated).

Unfortunately, while the characteristic inverted-cone resulting from down-dragging had been recorded, little is known about which pile installation technique was used on these sites in the past. It is therefore impossible to be sure, without going back to the original piling records (where they survive), whether such examples result from driving preformed piles. The pile excavated in Northampton was circular, and may not have been a preformed displacement pile. The same questions apply to Roman deposits at Vine Street in Leicester, which demonstrated similar sediment distortion associated with a circular concrete pile (Figure 51). The rough external surface of the pile suggests that it was a bored pile rather than a solid preformed pile, although it may have been installed

Figure 50: Section drawing showing sediment deformation adjacent to piles. © Worcestershire Archaeological Society and Worcestershire Historic Environment and Archaeology Service

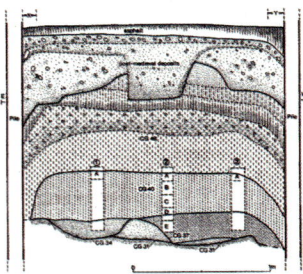

Figure 51: Layered deposits deformed by piling at Vine Street, Leicester. © University of Leicester Archaeological Services (ULAS)

with a temporary driven steel casing. It is therefore impossible to be sure, without going back to the original piling records (where they survive), whether such examples result from driven preformed piles.

Another example comes from Number 1 Poultry, London, where circular concrete piles installed in the 1970s were recorded during later excavation. Figure 52 shows a pile penetrating a Roman mosaic, which is undamaged outside the pile footprint (Rowsome 2000). The exact type of installation method is unknown, but again the surface finish of the piles is rough.

Figure 52: Pile and mosaic from No 1 Poultry. © MOLA

Figure 53: Impact of a driven pile on deposits at Finnegården 3A in Bergen, Norway, where dragged-down sediment layers and displaced wood are visible next to the pile. © Norwegian Directorate of Cultural Heritage

Waterlogged archaeological deposits are at great risk from driven piling, although much would seem to depend upon the orientation and state of preservation of surviving timberwork, in particular. Significant damage is reported from Finnegården 3A in Bergen, Norway (Biddle 1994) (Figure 53), and the Thames Exchange site, where waterfront timber revetments show damage up to three times the diameter of the pile (Nixon 1998, 42 and Figure 2). More limited deformation of deposits was reported by Stockwell (1984) from soft organic-rich deposits from Coppergate, where piles cleanly cut through waterlogged timber without significant levels of down dragging.

An ongoing project in The Netherlands to collect and assess images of past piling impacts has amassed an image library of around 10000 photographs showing piles on archaeological sites. Analysis of these images has yielded a similarly wide range of impact zones as described above, from little or no movement (seen in soft clay and peat soils) to large scale transformation witnessed in stiffer deposits, or where piles have encountered structural remains (Groenendijk *et al* 2016).

Engineering and field scale research

Down-dragging of sediment is also relevant to engineers, and several model-scale experiments have been carried out to characterise the extent of deformation. Most of these studies show a drop-off in visible sediment movement within about 1.5 pile diameters of the centre line of the pile (Hird *et al* 2006). This research was carried out predominantly on homogeneous clay soils, which may not effectively replicate all archaeological deposits. Model-scale (1:10) research on driven and CFA piles in layered soil has provided information on the mechanisms of sediment displacement and the extent of the impacts.

Figure 54 shows the typical extent of sediment distortion recorded in a model-scale experiment. Samples were tested in both consolidated and unconsolidated models, mostly with a clay layer sandwiched between two sand layers, with variable layer thickness and density. Some homogeneous samples with varying mixes of clay and sand, containing marker layers for identification of sediment displacement were also used (Figure 55).

Although a number of the tests in this work were on unconsolidated sediments (including both shown here), the results and data are physically and numerically similar to the tests on consolidated deposits that were also produced, and to the results from previous work (Hird and Moseley 2000). In almost all instances the maximum extent of deformation lies within 1.5 pile widths of the centre line of the pile, although 'most of the vertical displacement (or down-dragging of soil) is concentrated within a distance of 1 pile width from the pile centreline' (Hird *et al* 2006).

Field-scale evaluations have been carried out to test the extent of pile damage to archaeological deposits. At the JunXion, Lincoln, two 0.25m wide square preformed concrete displacement piles were installed

Figures 54 and 55: Typical result from model testing in layered ground, showing vertical displacement of the clay layer by the installation of a pile (Hird *et al* 2006 Figure 4.9) (top). Image of homogeneous sediment deformation, the composition of the sediment is 75% sand, with 25% kaolin clay. Marker layers are included to allow displacement to be recorded (bottom). © Keith Emmett

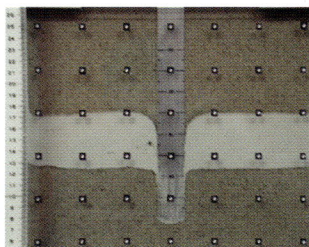

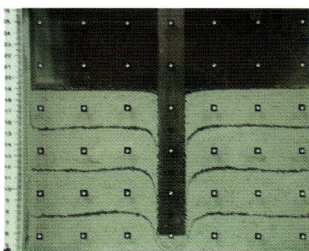

(one driven and one pre-augered then driven) and evaluation trenches excavated alongside to investigate the degree of sediment deformation. The excavation demonstrated that sediment deformation had occurred adjacent to the driven pile, but this was only visible within 0.1m of the pile edge (less than one pile width from the centreline). The down-dragging effect had nevertheless extended 1m down, clearly seen with different coloured material (see Figures 34 and 35). Other visible effects included cracking, remoulding of deposits and the creation of voids (Davies 2003). As the deposit was homogeneous fill deformation features were not particularly clear.

Excavations were also carried out beside four piles at Skirbeck Road, Boston, Lincolnshire. These included three preformed concrete piles (one of which was pre-augered, and another was fitted with a pointed shoe), and a hollow steel pile (see Figure 12). In all cases, sediment deformation was difficult to make out owing to the complicated nature of the stratigraphy. All of the visible impacts were within 1.5 pile widths of the pile centreline, and in several cases, significantly less (Rayner 2005).

Driven preformed piles: hydrogeological impacts

Model-scale tests suggest that there is no significant increase in permeability for driven piling in layered sand and clay samples, providing the impermeable (clay) layers are relatively soft and sufficiently thick, that is, more than two pile diameters thick. Changes do occur, however, where there is a thin clay layer relative to the pile diameter/width, which is exacerbated in the case of H-section piles (Hird *et al* 2006). These model-scale studies also demonstrate that small amounts of contaminants could be carried down at the pile toe but, in the absence of the creation of any long-term preferential pathways for further contamination, the impact that limited amounts of contaminant will have on archaeological deposits and artefacts is not likely to be excessive.

Excavations in Spurriergate, York have revealed extensive waterlogged deposits dating from the Roman and Anglo-Scandinavian periods. Much of the site had previously been piled using square-section preformed concrete piles. In one area of Roman dumping there was a clear zone of impact around each pile, and the sediments appeared much drier than the surrounding deposits. In another area, however, identical piles had been driven through a possible Anglo-Scandinavian timber building and organic-rich deposits showing no zone of impact around each pile. Equally, where concrete displacement piles were driven through Bronze Age timbers at Bramcote Green in London, the timbers were almost entirely destroyed; where there were no piles, the timbers were intact (T Nixon pers comm).

8.2 Small displacement pile impacts

Preformed steel

Figures 56 and 57: H-section pile showing re-entrant angle (top). © Trace Parts S.A. www.traceparts.com. H-section pile test with sand plugged within the flanges of the pile (Hird *et al* 2006 Figure 4.2a, bottom).

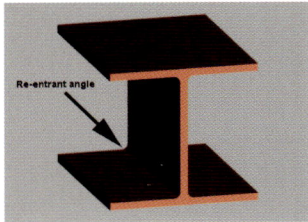

Although no field based evaluations of H-section piles have been carried out to assess potential impact on archaeological remains, some laboratory studies have been conducted. In model-scale tests with a clay layer between two sand layers, sand can be seen to plug within the re-entrant angles of the H-section pile and is carried down into, and possibly through, the clay layer (see Figures 56 and 57). This allows movement of liquid along the pile (Hird *et al* 2006). This partly confirms previous research on H-section piles (Hayman *et al* 1993; Boutwell *et al* 2000).

Another potential concern with steel piles is corrosion. A number of studies have been carried out on steel piles, which show very limited levels of corrosion occurring within the ground, within anoxic saturated soils (see for example reviews in Morley 1978 and in Tomlinson and Woodward 2008, Chapter 10, particularly 10.4). Fewer studies have looked in detail at the potential corrosion associated with soils above the groundwater table. Where data exist, corrosion appears to be enhanced in disturbed soils with fluctuating soil moisture / oxygen content and also on contaminated sites. It is possible that corrosion of metal piles may damage archaeological materials when corrosion products are transported into other parts of the deposit in solution through surface water/groundwater percolation, although the risk is fairly low. The use of plastic sheeting or pre-treatment of metal piles would avoid issues associated with pile corrosion.

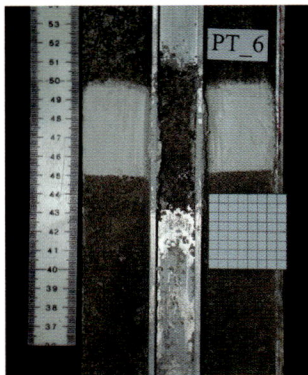

8.3 Supported non-displacement (bored) pile impacts

Temporarily supported bore: physical impacts

Figure 58: Loss of material during bored piling operations at the level of the watertable, at Number 1 Poultry, London. © MOLA

In excavations next to new piles installed at Number 1 Poultry, about 7% of the bored piles had caused significant damage at the point at which they encountered the water table, with an area twice the diameter of the pile being affected (Nixon 1998, 41). This may have occurred during the installation of the pile casing as the damage was only seen next to (some of) the supported non-displacement piles, but not next to unsupported CFA piles (T Nixon pers comm). The impact is shown in Figure 58, with loss of an area of beaten earth floor (the yellow-coloured deposit) adjacent to the pile (Rowsome 2000).

8.4 Unsupported non-displacement CFA pile impacts

Continuous flight auger (CFA): physical impacts

The impacts of CFA piles have been investigated by model-scale research (Hird *et al* 2006; 2011; Ni *et al* 2010). These demonstrated that impacts outside the diameter of the pile were relatively small, compared with those recorded in model-scale driven circular, square- and H-section piles.

Figure 59: Model piles in transparent soil. © Ni Qing

This is shown in Figure 59, in which piles are inserted into a transparent medium which replicates the properties of a soft clay soil. Particles of mica are illuminated by a laser, and when they move due to soil displacement, this movement is captured by digital camera, the distance they have moved is calculated and indicated with a yellow arrow. The image of the driven pile on the left (a) clearly shows evidence of sediment movement. Very limited movement is detected in middle image (b) which represents a well-constructed CFA pile. The image on the right (c) shows what happens if the auger is flighted. In this case when the rotation speed was doubled halfway through insertion, the ground was drawn towards the auger.

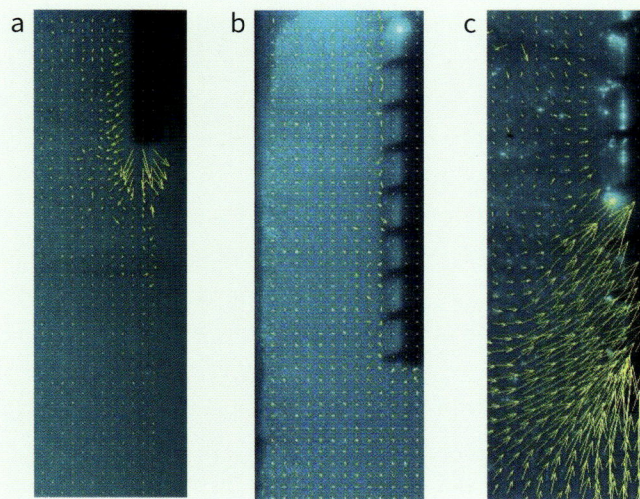

Figure 60: Pile installed into pre-augered hole at Skirbeck Road, Boston. The installation has not deformed the layers, and the edge of the borehole can be seen to the left of the pile. © APS

Aside from model-scale observations, some field-scale analysis of auger impacts has been undertaken, in both cases to assess whether pre-augering driven pile locations was an effective way to measure vertical sediment displacement (Davies 2003; Rayner 2005). As can be seen in Figure 60 there was no impact outside the diameter of the auger.

9   Glossary

anoxic used to refer to a deposit in which oxygen is virtually absent

aquitard an impermeable layer restricting groundwater flow between aquifers

arisings spoil generated and brought up through groundworks/drilling

bentonite an absorbent clay mineral used in slurry form as a drilling mud. It has a specific gravity of about 1.2 thus is sufficient to stop water and soil ingress

casing generally a tube used to line the pile hole; usually of metal and removed following piling

cathodic protection an electrochemical process used to protect metals from corrosion in water/aquatic environments

cohesive/cohesionless soils terms used to refer to firm or loose soils, ie clay rich (cohesive) or gravel (cohesionless)

deformation generally used to refer to a change in shape, in this case, usually to a soil or sediment, resulting from applied force

displacement generally lateral movement of soil during insertion of a pile

drilling fluids used to aid the drilling process, often a form of slurry, bentonite or even water

end bearing a piling system where most of the load is carried by the base (end) of the pile

exothermic a chemical reaction which produces heat

helical a helical pile is corkscrew shaped; a central bar with a series of pitched plates attached

high slump concrete has a high water to cement ratio, making it a highly workable material

hydraulic conductivity is a measure of the way and speed water passes through soils/other mediums

Hz Hertz

kentledge a form of incremental pile loading used for testing piling

kN = a kilonewton. A Newton is the force required to accelerate 1kg mass at $1m/s^2$. An apple exerts a force of approximately one Newton, and a mass of one tonne equates to 10kN in the Earth's gravity field.

particle velocity the velocity at which the ground vibrates. It is measured in millimetres per second. Peak particle velocity has been accepted as an important indicator of structural damage

perched (water table) water held above the real water table, usually through the presence of an impermeable layer

Plunge piles are a type of bored pile used where basement excavation takes place at the same time as the construction of the superstructure. The concrete pile is cast to the level of the basement, and a steel column / liner provides the link between the cast pile and the ground floor slab

secant technically a line passing through two points of a curve – in this case, a secant wall is a line of intercutting piles

shear strength this is the maximum stress which can be sustained before a material will rupture, or fail in shear

sleeving a casing for the pile, generally permanently left in the ground; can be paper, metal, plastic etc; sometimes used for guidance during drilling

statnamic a rapid load testing method for piles which may be used as an alternative to static or dynamic tests

tie-back an anchorage or the tie rod connected to it which may be used to support walls and other structures

underream an enlarged pedestal cut out of the soil at the base of a pile. This is usually done with a cutting tool, which can be expanded and rotated at the base of the pile shaft

unstable soils sands and gravels which are not self-supporting and therefore liable to collapse into a bored hole

10 References

APABE 2017 *Guidance for best practice for treatment of human remains excavated from Christian burial grounds in England*. London: Advisory Panel on the Archaeology of Burials in England.

Biddle, M. 1994 'What Future for British Archaeology', the opening address at the Eighth Annual Conference of the Institute of Field Archaeologists, Bradford 13-15 April 1994. *Archaeology in Britain Conference 1994*. Oxford: Oxbow Books

Boutwell, G P Nataraj, M S and McManis, K L 2000 'Deep foundations on brownfield sites'. Prague 2000 conference, Prague

British Standard 2009 *Code of practice for noise and vibration control on construction and open sites – Part 2: Vibration* BS 5228-2

British Standard 1990 *Evaluation and measurement for vibration in buildings – Part 1: Guide for measurement of vibrations and evaluation of their effects on buildings* BS 7385-1

British Standard 1993 *Evaluation and measurement for vibration in buildings - Part 2: Guide to damage levels from groundborne vibration* BS 7385-2

Burland, J, Chapman, T, Skinner, H, Brown, M, (eds) 2012 *ICE Manual of Geotechnical Engineering Volume II*. London: Institution of Civil Engineers.

Butcher, A P, Powell, J J M and Skinner, H D, (eds) 2006a *Reuse of Foundations for Urban Sites, a Best Practice Handbook*. Bracknall: IHS BRE Press

Butcher, A P, Powell, J J M and Skinner, H D, (eds) 2006b *Re-use of Foundations for Urban Sites*, Proceedings of the International Conference. Bracknall: IHS BRE Press

Chapman, T; Anderson S; Windle J 2007 *Reuse of foundations (C653)*. London: CIRIA

Corfield, M, Hinton, P, Nixon, T and Pollard, M (eds) 1998 Preserving Archaeological Remains *in situ: Proceedings of the Conference of 1st-3rd April 1996*. London: Museum of London Archaeology Service

City of London 2017 'Archaeology and Development Guidance SPD'. Accessed online (1/3/19) at: https://www.cityoflondon.gov.uk/services/environment-and-planning/planning/heritage-and-design/Documents/arch-dev-guidance-spd.pdf

Dalwood, C H, Buteux, V A and Darlington, J 1994 'Excavations at Farrier Street and other sites north of the city wall, Worcester 1988-92'. *Trans Worcestershire Archaeol Soc* 3rd Series 14, 75-114

Davies, G 2003 'Archaeological Field Evaluation of the Impacts of Piling at The JunXion, St Marks Street, Lincoln'. ARCUS: Report No 750.1: unpublished – 2004 'Interim Report on the Impact of Piling on Archaeological Deposits'. ARCUS Report No 711.1: unpublished

Davis, M J, Gdaniec, K L A, Bryce, M and White, L 2004 *Study of the Mitigation of Construction Impacts on Archaeological Remains.* London: Museum of London Archaeology Service

Department of Environment 1990 Planning *Policy Guidance Note 16: Archaeology and Planning.* London: HMSO

DIN (German Standards Institution: Deutsche Industrie-Norm, B 1970 'Vibrations in buildings'. Unpublished draft

Edwards, R 1998 'The effects of changes in groundwater on the survival of buried metal artefacts', in M Corfield, P Hinton, T Nixon and M Pollard (eds) *Preserving Archaeological Remains* in situ:. *Proceedings of the Conference of 1st-3rd April 1996.* London: Museum of London Archaeology Service, 86-92

Environment Agency 2001 *Piling and Penetrative Ground Improvement Methods on Land Affected by Contamination: Guidance on Pollution Prevention.* NGWCLC Report NC/99/73

Federation of Piling Specialists (FPS) 2006 *Handbook on Pile Load Testing.* Beckenham: FPS

Groenendijk, M., Kars, H. and Huisman, D.J. (2016) Between the Piles. Studying Excavation Photographs to Determine the Area of Physical Disturbance Caused by Piling in the Netherlands, *Conservation and Management of Archaeological Sites*, 18:1-3, 59-69, DOI: 10.1080/13505033.2016.1181933

Hayman, J W, Adams, R B and Adams, R G 1993 'Foundation piling as a potential conduit for DNAPL migration', *in Proceedings of the Air and Waste Management Association Meeting.* Denver

Head, J M and Jardine, F M 1992 *Ground-borne Vibrations Arising from Piling.* London: Construction Industry Research and Information Association

Hird, C C, Emmett, K B and Davies, G 2006 *Piling in Layered Ground: Risks to Groundwater and Archaeology.* Environment Agency Science Report SC020074/SR. Bristol: Environment Agency

Hird, C C and Moseley, V J 2000 'Model study of smear zones around vertical drains in layered soil'. *Geotechnique* 50, 89-97

Hird, C C, Ni, Q., and Guymer, I. 2011 Physical modelling of deformations around piling augers in clay. *Geotechnique* 61, No. 11, 993-999, http://dx.doi.org/10.1680/geot.9.T.028

Historic England 2016 Preserving Archaeology Remains, Decision-taking for sites under development. Swindon: Historic England

Hughes, R, Coles, B and Henley, R 2004 'The reuse of pile locations at Governor's House development site, City of London', in T Nixon *Preserving Archaeological Remains* in situ*? Proceedings of the 2nd Conference, 12-14 September 2001.* London: Museum of London Archaeology Service, 98-104

Matthiesen, H 2005 *Influence from piling on cultural deposits at Bryggen, Bergen. Report to Riksantikvaren, Norway.* National Museum of Denmark, Department of Conservation, Report no 10832-0007-1

Matthiesen, H. and Gregory, D. Eds. 2012 Preserving Archaeological Remains *in situ*, proceedings of the fourth international conference. Special edition of *Conservation and Management of Archaeological Sites.* 14 (1-4)

McDaid, M 2006a *Lincoln Cathedral Street, Lincoln*. Archaeological Watching Brief. LAS Report 864 – 2006b Lincoln College, Monks Road, Lincoln. Archaeological Watching Brief. LAS Report 902

MHCLG – Ministry of Housing, Communities and Local Government 2018 National Planning Policy Framework. London: MHCLG. Accessed online (1/3/19) at: https://www.gov.uk/government/publications/national-planning-policy-framework--2

Mitchell, J and Jardine, F M 2002 *A guide to Ground Treatment*. London: CIRIA

Morley, J 1978 *A Review of the Underground Corrosion of Steel Piling*. British Steel Corporation

Ni, Q., Hird, C C and Guymer, I. (2010). Physical modelling of pile penetration in clay using transparent soil and particle image velocimetry. *Geotechnique* 60, No. 2, 121-132, doi: 10.1680/geot.8.P.052

Nixon, T 1998 'Practically preserved: observations on the impact of construction on urban archaeological deposits', in M Corfield, P Hinton, T Nixon and M Pollard (eds) *Preserving Archaeological Remains* in situ. *Proceedings of the Conference of 1st-3rd April 1996*. London: Museum of London Archaeology Service, 39-46

Nixon, T (ed) 2004 *Preserving Archaeological Remains* in situ. *Proceedings of the 2nd Conference, 12-14 September 2001*. London: Museum of London Archaeology Service

Northamptonshire Archaeology (undated) 'Archaeological evaluation at Barclaycard, Marefair, Northampton, Stage 2: trial excavation'

Ove Arup and Partners and York University in association with Bernard Thorpe 1991 'York Development and Archaeology Study'

Rayner, T 2005 'Archaeological investigations and watching brief on land at Skirbeck Road, Boston, Lincolnshire (BSR04)'. Archaeological Project Services (APS) Report No. 20/05: unpublished

Rowsome, P 2000 *Heart of the City: Roman, Medieval and Modern London Revealed by Archaeology at 1 Poultry*. London: Museum of London Archaeology Service

Sheward, T 2003 'Screw piling in Salisbury'. *New Steel Construction* (November/December): 27-8

Shilston, D T and Fletcher, S L 1998 'Geotechnical engineering for the in-situ preservation of archaeological remains', in M Corfield, P Hinton, T Nixon and M Pollard (eds) *Preserving Archaeological Remains* in situ. *Proceedings of the Conference of 1st-3rd April 1996.* London: Museum of London Archaeological Service, 8-15

Sidell, E J, Higuchi, T, Allison, RJ and Long, AJ 2004 'The response of archaeological sediments and artefacts to imposed stress regimes as a consequence of past, present and future anthropogenic activity', *in* Nixon, T (ed) *Preserving Archaeological Remains* in situ*? Proceedings of the 2nd Conference 12-14 September 2001*. London: Museum of London Archaeology Service, 42-9

Steel Piling Group (SPG) 2018 *Installation Plant Overview*. www.steelpilinggroup. org/guidance/

Stockwell, M 1984 'Foundation preparation and the archaeologist', in P V Addyman and B V E (eds) *Archaeological Papers from York Presented to M W Barley*. York, 158-62

Tomlinson, M J and Woodward, J. 1994 *Pile Design and Construction Practice* (5th edn). Abingdon: Taylor and Francis

Westcott, F J, Smith, J W N and Lean, C M B (2003) Piling in contaminated ground: environmental impacts, regulatory concerns and effective solutions. Engineering Geology 70: 259-268.

Williams, J 2006 'Pile re-use at The Collection, Lincoln: lessons learnt', in A P Butcher, J J M Powell and H D Skinner *Reuse of Foundations for Urban Sites, Proceedings of the International Conference*. Bracknall: IHS BRE Press, 303-7

Williams, J and Butcher, A P 2006 'Foundation re-use as a mechanism for the preservation of buried cultural heritage in urban centres: how new engineering research helps limit archaeological damage', in *Proceedings of the 7th European Conference 'Sauveur' Safeguarded Cultural Heritage, Understanding and Viability for the Enlarged Europe, Prague 31st May-3rd June 2006*.

Williams, J., Hunter, R., Branch, N., Swindle, G., Walsh, N., Valcarez, I., Palmer, A., Langdale-Smith, T. and Allen, M. (2008) Monitoring leaching from cast *in situ* piles. In H. Kars and R. M. van Heeringen, Eds. Preserving Archaeological Remains *In Situ*, Proceedings of the Third International Conference (Geoarchaeological and Bioarchaeological Studies 10). Amsterdam: Vrije Universiteit Amsterdam, 175-180.

11 Acknowledgements

Contributors

This document was revised as a collaborative writing exercise by the following individuals:

Andrew Armstrong, Chris Barker, Richard Buckley, Mike Collins, Sophie Jackson, Alastair McIntosh, Matt Nicholas, Chris Oram, Chris Robinson, Jane Sidell, Kathryn Stubbs, Tony Suckling, Rosy Szymanski, Jim Williams, Helen Woodhouse.

Images

All images © Historic England unless specified below.

Figures 1, 22, 27, 47-49, 52: © University of Leicester Archaeological Services (ULAS)

Figures 6-8: © Roger Bullivant Limited

Figures 9-10, 14-17, 28: © Cementation Foundations Skanska:

Figures 11, 39: © Pre-construct Archaeology

Figures 18, 31, 40, 42-46, 53, 59: © MOLA

Figures 19-21: © Keller Ground Engineering

Figures 23, 36: © Tim Sheward

Figure 24: © Mark Allen

Figures 29-30: © Mike Brown

Figure 32: Courtesy of RuFUS Consortium 2006

Figure 34: © ARCUS

Figure 35: Davies 2003

Contact Historic England

**East of England
Regional Office**
Brooklands
24 Brooklands Avenue
Cambridge CB2 8BU
Tel: 01223 582749
Email: eastofengland@
HistoricEngland.org.uk

Fort Cumberland
Fort Cumberland Road
Eastney
Portsmouth PO4 9LD
Tel: 023 9285 6704
Email: fort.
cumberland@
HistoricEngland.org.uk

**London & South East
Regional Office**
4th Floor
Cannon Bridge House
25 Dowgate Hill
London EC4R 2YA
Tel: 020 7973 3700
Email: london@
HistoricEngland.org.uk
or southeast@
HistoricEngland.org.uk

**Midlands
Regional Office**
The Axis
10 Holliday Street
Birmingham B1 1TF
Tel: 0121 625 6870
Email: eastmidlands@
HistoricEngland.org.uk
or westmidlands@
HistoricEngland.org.uk

**North East & Yorkshire
Regional Offices**
Newcastle
Bessie Surtees House
41-44 Sandhill
Newcastle Upon
Tyne NE1 3JF
Tel: 0191 269 1255
Email: northeast@
HistoricEngland.org.uk

York
37 Tanner Row
York YO1 6WP
Tel: 01904 601948
Email: yorkshire@
HistoricEngland.org.uk

**North West
Regional Office**
3rd Floor,
Canada House
3 Chepstow Street
Manchester M1 5FW
Tel: 0161 242 1416
Email: northwest@
HistoricEngland.org.uk

**South West
Regional Office**
29 Queen Square
Bristol BS1 4ND
Tel: 0117 975 1308
Email: southwest@
HistoricEngland.org.uk

Swindon
The Engine House
Fire Fly Avenue
Swindon SN2 2EH
Tel: 01793 445050
Email: swindon@
HistoricEngland.org.uk